英语 2 同步练习（基础模块）

主　编　黄静静　周巍巍　范复旺
副主编　怀瑞娟　郭亚辉　法　磊

北京理工大学出版社
BEIJING INSTITUTE OF TECHNOLOGY PRESS

版权专有　侵权必究

图书在版编目(CIP)数据

英语 2 同步练习：基础模块 / 黄静静，周巍巍，范复旺主编. --北京：北京理工大学出版社，2023.3
　ISBN 978-7-5763-2233-0

Ⅰ.①英… Ⅱ.①黄… ②周… ③范… Ⅲ.①英语课-中等专业学校-教学参考资料 Ⅳ.①G634.413

中国国家版本馆 CIP 数据核字(2023)第 060010 号

出版发行 / 北京理工大学出版社有限责任公司
社　　址 / 北京市海淀区中关村南大街 5 号
邮　　编 / 100081
电　　话 / (010)68914775(总编室)
　　　　　 (010)82562903(教材售后服务热线)
　　　　　 (010)68944723(其他图书服务热线)
网　　址 / http://www.bitpress.com.cn
经　　销 / 全国各地新华书店
印　　刷 / 涿州汇美亿浓印刷有限公司
开　　本 / 787 毫米×1092 毫米　1/16
印　　张 / 11　　　　　　　　　　　　　　　　　责任编辑 / 王晓莉
字　　数 / 233 千字　　　　　　　　　　　　　　文案编辑 / 王晓莉
版　　次 / 2023 年 3 月第 1 版　2023 年 3 月第 1 次印刷　责任校对 / 周瑞红
定　　价 / 38.00 元　　　　　　　　　　　　　　责任印制 / 边心超

图书出现印装质量问题,请拨打售后服务热线,本社负责调换

前　言

　　本书依据《中等职业学校英语课程标准（2020年版）》，以国家教育部指定的"十四五"职业教育国家规划教材《英语1基础模块》《英语2基础模块》《英语拓展模块》为主要参考教材，结合中等职业学校就业与升学的实际情况而编写。

　　本书在编写过程中与"十四五"职业教育国家规划英语教材紧密联系，能够夯实学生的英语学习基础，适用于所有中职学生的英语学习。共分为8个单元，每个单元所附的习题，以 Warming up、Listening and Speaking、Reading and Writing、Grammar 以及 For Better Performance 五个模块的形式展开，呈现方式多样化，以语音、填空、选择、对话练习、完形填空、阅读理解、改错及写作的练习方式帮助学生掌握词汇、课文内容和语法知识，使其拓展知识面，提高英语水平。针对学生高考的需求，在每个单元的学习内容结束后，本书又附有单元检测习题，习题内容符合对口英语高考大纲，且题型与高考题型一致，能有效地达到举一反三、灵活运用所学知识点的目的，可以帮助学生在日常学习中巩固基础、提高技能。本书很好地满足了职业学校的学生参加职教高考的需求。

　　我们本着"注重基础，突出运用，精选内容，强化训练，提高分数"的原则，力争做到"由浅入深、循序渐进"，符合中等职业学校学生的认知特点和接受能力。本书可作为中等职业学校教师的复习教学用书，也可作为一、二年级学生日常学习用书，而对于参加对口升学的毕业班学生来说，其同样适用。

　　本书的作者均是来自教学一线、有多年教学经验的教师。但由于水平有限，疏漏与不足之处在所难免，恳请各位老师、同学及其他读者批评指正。

编　者

目 录

Unit 1　Travel 1
　　Warming-up 1
　　Listening and Speaking 2
　　Reading and Writing 4
　　Grammar 6
　　For Better Performance 10
　　单元检测 11

Unit 2　Health and Fitness 21
　　Warming-up 21
　　Listening and Speaking 22
　　Reading and Writing 23
　　Grammar 26
　　For Better Performance 29
　　单元检测 31

Unit 3　Internship 40
　　Warming-up 40
　　Listening and Speaking 41
　　Reading and Writing 43
　　Grammar 45
　　For Better Performance 48
　　单元检测 50

Unit 4　Volunteer Work 59
　　Warming-up 59
　　Listening and Speaking 60
　　Reading and Writing 61
　　Grammar 64

For Better Performance ………………………………………………………… 67
    单元检测 …………………………………………………………………………… 68

Unit 5　Ancient Civilization ………………………………………………… 77
    Warming-up ……………………………………………………………………… 77
    Listening and Speaking ………………………………………………………… 78
    Reading and Writing …………………………………………………………… 80
    Grammar ………………………………………………………………………… 82
    For Better Performance ………………………………………………………… 87
    单元检测 …………………………………………………………………………… 88

Unit 6　Craftsmanship ……………………………………………………… 97
    Warming-up ……………………………………………………………………… 97
    Listening and Speaking ………………………………………………………… 98
    Reading and Writing …………………………………………………………… 100
    Grammar ………………………………………………………………………… 103
    For Better Performance ………………………………………………………… 106
    单元检测 …………………………………………………………………………… 107

Unit 7　Invention and Innovation ………………………………………… 116
    Warming-up ……………………………………………………………………… 116
    Listening and Speaking ………………………………………………………… 117
    Reading and Writing …………………………………………………………… 118
    Grammar ………………………………………………………………………… 122
    For Better Performance ………………………………………………………… 125
    单元检测 …………………………………………………………………………… 126

Unit 8　Green Earth ………………………………………………………… 136
    Warming-up ……………………………………………………………………… 136
    Listening and Speaking ………………………………………………………… 137
    Reading and Writing …………………………………………………………… 138
    Grammar ………………………………………………………………………… 141
    For Better Performance ………………………………………………………… 144
    单元检测 …………………………………………………………………………… 146

Unit 1

Travel

Warming-up

一、句型汇总

1. Shangri-La is famous for the Pudacuo National Park. 香格里拉以普达措国家公园而闻名。

2. It's really worth visiting. 这里真是值得一游。

3. Shangri-La is also rich in ethnic culture. 香格里拉还有丰富的民族文化。

4. I'd like to book a non-smoking double room... 我想预定一个无烟的双人间。

5. By the way, what's the room rate? 顺便问一句,房间定价多少?

6. We'll be there in 20 minutes. 我们20分钟后就到。

二、英汉互译

1. avoid (v.) _____
2. 令人舒服的 (adj.) _____
3. 敬业 (n.) _____ →致力于 (v.) _____
4. discover (v.) _____ →发现 (n.) _____
5. 王朝 (n.) _____
6. 了不起 (adj.) _____
7. 全国的 (adj.) _____ →民族、国家 (n.) _____
8. 产品 (n.) _____ →produce (v.) _____

9. reservation (*n.*) _____ →预订 (*v.*) _____

10. 独特的 (*adj.*) _____   11. vegetation (*n.*) _____

12. 经历 (*v.*) _____ →有经验的 (*adj.*) _____

Listening and Speaking

一、找出与所给单词画线部分读音相同的选项

(　　) 1. ag<u>a</u>ency　　A. n<u>a</u>tional　　B. <u>a</u>void　　C. lugg<u>a</u>ge　　D. m<u>a</u>jor

(　　) 2. <u>c</u>omfortable　　A. <u>a</u>gency　　B. experien<u>c</u>e　　C. ethni<u>c</u>　　D. Fran<u>c</u>e

(　　) 3. <u>e</u>thnic　　A. thr<u>ou</u>ghout　　B. t<u>o</u>gether　　C. th<u>e</u>re　　D. th<u>o</u>se

(　　) 4. <u>t</u>icket　　A. devo<u>t</u>ion　　B. educa<u>t</u>ion　　C. e<u>t</u>hnic　　D. reserva<u>t</u>ion

(　　) 5. sugges<u>tion</u>　　A. op<u>tion</u>　　B. reserva<u>tion</u>　　C. vegeta<u>tion</u>　　D. ques<u>tion</u>

二、情景交际的单项选择题

(　　) 1. —Shall I help you with the suitcase?

—_____

A. It's all right, thanks.　　B. Yes, go ahead, please.

C. I don't want to trouble you.　　D. No, please don't do it.

(　　) 2. —Can I have a look at your passport, please?

—_____

A. I can't agree with you.　　B. Don't mention it.

C. I'm sorry to hear that.　　D. Sure, here you are.

(　　) 3. — Excuse me. Could you tell me where the reading room is?

—_____ I didn't hear clearly.

A. Pardon me.　　B. Sure.　　C. Yes, please.　　D. How are you?

(　　) 4. —What time will you arrive, sir?

—_____

A. For two hours.　　B. Around six in the evening.

C. Since 6 pm.　　D. About 2 kilometers.

(　　) 5. —By the way, what's the room rate?

—_____

A. Room 201.　　B. On the third floor.

C. It's big enough.　　D. 380 *yuan* a night.

三、用所给句子补全下面对话

A：May I help you, sir?

B：My wife and I want to see the places of interest in Handan. 1

A：Certainly. Handan is called "the hometown of idioms". There are many scenic spots in Handan. 2

B：Well, only two days.

A：Oh, I'm afraid two days isn't enough for you to see all the places of interest here. 3   It is a general tour of the city.

B： 4

A：A great many. Jingniang Lake, Toddler Bridge, Congtai Park, Fuyang Park, Nanhu Park and Fuyang River.

B： 5   How much is the tour?

A：300 *yuan* for each person.

B：OK, thank you.

> A. How long would you like to stay in our city?
> B. Can you arrange a tour for us?
> C. Why not take a look at this two-day package tour.
> D. I'm wondering what attractions are included in the tour?
> E. Sounds great.

四、场景模拟

编写一组对话,你作为一个导游,引领外国朋友参观你家乡的旅游景点。

提示句型：1. Welcome to… 2. Can I help you, Madam?

3. I'm interested in… 4. I'm searching for…

5. I'm wondering… 6. Why not take a look at…

Reading and Writing

一、用括号内所给汉语提示或单词的适当形式填空

1. Xu Xiake is a famous _____（地理学家）in the Ming Dynasty.
2. He experienced all sorts of difficulties and _____（困苦）.
3. Xu Xiake never thought of _____（quit）.
4. Xu Xiake spent over 30 years _____（travel）throughout the country.
5. He recorded his _____（经历）and discoveries carefully in his diary.
6. Due to his _____（devote）, the diary eventually became *The Travel Notes of Xu Xiake*.
7. Our flight _____（最终）left five hours late.
8. He _____（避免）comfortable travel options and chose to go almost everywhere on foot.
9. Marco Polo _____（花费）24 years traveling and he set out his first trip at 17.
10. When he was 19, his father _____（去世）and he had to take care of his mother.

二、完形填空

Modern life is impossible without __1__. The fastest way to travel is by plane. With a modern plane, you can travel in one day to places which it took a month or more __2__ to one hundred years ago.

Travelling by train is __3__ than travelling by plane, but you can see beautiful places __4__ the windows. Modern trains have __5__ seats and dining-cars. They make the long journey pleasant.

Some people prefer to travel by sea. Ships are not __6__ trains or planes, but travelling by sea is a very pleasant way __7__ a holiday.

Many people like to travel by car. You can travel three or __8__ miles or only fifty miles a day, just as you like. You can stop anytime if there is __9__ to see. That is __10__ travelling by car is popular for pleasure trips, while people usually take a train or a plane for business trips.

( ) 1. A. travelling   B. travel   C. travelled   D. traveller
( ) 2. A. to getting   B. to get   C. get   D. got
( ) 3. A. slower   B. slowest   C. slowly   D. more slow
( ) 4. A. in   B. throughout   C. from   D. through
( ) 5. A. comfort   B. comfortable   C. uncomfortable   D. comfortably

( )6. A. so fast as   B. as quickly as   C. too fast as   D. so faster as
( )7. A. to spend   B. in spend   C. spending   D. to spending
( )8. A. four hundreds   B. four hundred   C. hundreds of   D. four hundreds of
( )9. A. interested   B. nothing interesting
　　C. interesting something   D. something interesting
( )10. A. what   B. that   C. why   D. which

三、阅读理解

阅读下面短文,从每题所给的 A、B、C、D 四个选项中选出最佳答案。

Do you like to travel? There are several ways you can find out about the countries and places you wish to visit. You can talk to friends who have travelled to the places, or you can read travel books.

It appears that there are three types of travel books. The first are those books that give a personal idea of travels which the writers has got himself. These books can be useful if the writers share their travelling experiences with others. The second kind are those books which give objective (客观的) information of things to be done and seen. If a person who has a good education has written such a book about the facts of a place, then it is more useful. The third kind are those books which are called "a guide" to some place or other. If they are good, they will describe and explain the place in detail. Like the first kind, they can be interesting and exciting, but their main purpose is to help the reader plan his travel in the most helpful way.

Whatever kind of travel book you choose, you must make sure that the book does not describe everything as interesting, exciting or fantastic. You must also keep an open eye on its date of publication because travel is a very helpful matter and many things change quickly. Finally, you should make sure that it's easy to find the useful information for your travel.

( )1. The first paragraph mainly talks about _____.
　　A. why you want to know a country or a place of interest
　　B. how you learn about the countries and places you want to visit
　　C. the best way to learn about a country is to read travel books
　　D. what you want to know if you wish to travel

( )2. How many kinds of travel books did the writer show?
　　A. Four.   B. Three.   C. Two.   D. Only one.

( )3. Travellers can get the most help from _____ of travel books before planning their trip.
　　A. the first kind   B. the second kind

     C. the third kind   D. every kind

( )4. Which of the following is NOT TRUE according to the passage?

    A. The writer of the first kind of travel books gives his ideas after he travels.

    B. The second kind of travel books may give you objective facts about the place.

    C. There are two things you should pay attention to when choosing a travel book.

    D. The third kind are those books which are called "a guide" to some place or other.

( )5. The date of publication must be noticed because _____.

    A. the writers of travel books may be different

    B. the information in travel books is always changing

    C. not all travel books can describe everything as very interesting

    D. it's easy to find the useful information for your travel

四、书面表达

题目：An unforgettable trip

词数要求：80~100 词

写作要求：1. 写一次让你难忘的旅行；

     2. 它为什么会让你难忘。

Grammar

一、从下面每小题四个选项中选出最佳选项

( )1. —Where _____ Allison go on vacation last summer?

   —She _____ to Australia.

   A. did; went   B. does; went   C. did; go   D. do; go

( )2. Some fish _____ out of the water just now.
   A. jumps   B. jumped   C. are jumping   D. will jump

( )3. —Millie, where is your mother?
   —She _____ too late last night, so she is still sleeping in her bedroom.
   A. works   B. worked   C. will work   D. is working

( )4. The poor boy _____ a lot of money, but he didn't _____ it.
   A. received; receive   B. accepted; accept
   C. received; accept   D. accepted; receive

( )5. The little girl looked as if she _____ cry.
   A. was about   B. was about to
   C. is about to   D. is about

( )6. It rained hard yesterday, so I _____ at home.
   A. have to stay   B. had to stay   C. have stay   D. has stay

( )7. He _____ make a home page three years ago, but now he is good at it.
   A. can   B. can't   C. could   D. couldn't

( )8. When he was 19, his father _____ and he had to take care of his mother.
   A. died   B. dead   C. death   D. dying

( )9. However, Xu Xiake didn't _____ his dream of traveling.
   A. give up   B. gives up   C. giving up   D. gave up

( )10. With the support of his family, Xu Xiake set off for the first time at 22 and _____ four major trips in his lifetime.
   A. took   B. takes   C. taken   D. taking

( )11. Xu Xiake _____ in books about different places at an early age.
   A. be interested   B. became interested
   C. become interest   D. became interest

( )12. A pair of glasses _____ broken just now.
   A. was   B. were   C. are   D. is

( )13. Tom and Mary _____ China last month.
   A. come to   B. came to   C. come   D. came

( )14. Mike _____ to bed until 12 o'clock last night, so I _____ up late.
   A. didn't go; got   B. didn't went; get
   C. Wasn't go; got   D. doesn't went; get

( )15. Mary _____ English yesterday morning.
    A. reads   B. readed   C. read   D. reading

( )16. There _____ no one here a moment ago.
    A. was   B. were   C. is   D. are

( )17. I listened but _____ nothing.
    A. hear   B. hearing   C. heard   D. heart

( )18. My sister watches TV every evening, but she _____ TV last night.
    A. watches   B. wasn't watched
    C. didn't watch   D. didn't watched

( )19. Mr. Green with his wife _____ sitting there when I came in.
    A. is   B. was   C. are   D. were

( )20. My mother _____ housework yesterday.
    A. didn't   B. didn't do   C. wasn't do   D. doesn't do

( )21. —_____ you like the book? —No, I didn't. I _____ like it at all.
    A. Did; didn't   B. Do; don't
    C. Were; don't   D. Were; wasn't

( )22. It _____ the Americans about five days to _____ there in 1959.
    A. takes; get to   B. took; get
    C. takes; get   D. took; get to

( )23. We _____ the mountains for several times last year.
    A. climbed   B. climb   C. were climbing   D. had climbed

( )24. Tom cleaned his room and _____ his clothes on Sunday.
    A. wash   B. washing   C. were washed   D. washed

( )25. David has worked here for ten years since he _____ from university.
    A. graduate   B. has graduated   C. graduated   D. graduating

( )26. —Who locked the door yesterday.
    —_____
    A. I do   B. I did   C. I will   D. I can

( )27. —You look tired. I wonder _____ last night.
    —I didn't go to bed until 11 for preparing a report.
    A. when you go to bed   B. when you went to bed
    C. when did you go to bed   D. when did you went to bed

( )28. —Helen has gone to Beijing on business.
　　　—Oh, I didn't know. When _____?
　　　A. did he leave　　　　　　　B. he left
　　　C. does he leave　　　　　　D. was he leaving

( )29. —What delicious fish it is!
　　　—My mother _____ it for me by herself.
　　　A. cooked　　B. cooks　　C. cooking　　D. was cooked

( )30. —Whose is this lovely toy panda?
　　　—It's mine. My brother _____ it as a gift on my birthday.
　　　A. gives　　B. giving　　C. was gave　　D. gave

二、找出下列句子中错误的选项，并改正过来

1. How is Jane's sister yesterday evening?
　　A B　　C　　　　　D

2. He goes to school by bike last week.
　　　A　　　　　B　　C　　D

3. Thomas can fly kites when he was seven years old.
　　　　　A　　　B　　　C　　　　　D

4. Did you saw him just now?
　　A　　B　　C　　D

5. Bill wasn't watch TV last night.
　　　A　　　B　　C　D

6. I didn't my homework yesterday because of my fever.
　　A　　　B　　　　　　　　C　　　　　D

7. I looked around but find nothing and nobody in the room.
　　　A　　　　B　　C　　　　　　　　D

8. What was he do when I was not at home last weekend?
　　　A　B　　　　　　C　D

9. Six years has passed since we have entered Handan vocational school.
　　　A　　B　　　　C　　　D

10. It was reported that Shenzhou XIII safely lands on earth on April 16, 2022.
　　　　　A　　　　　　　　　　　B　　C　　　　D

1.( )应为_____　2.( )应为_____　3.( )应为_____
4.( )应为_____　5.( )应为_____　6.( )应为_____
7.( )应为_____　8.( )应为_____　9.( )应为_____
10.( )应为_____

For Better Performance

一、找出与所给单词画线部分读音相同的选项

( ) 1. l<u>u</u>ggage   A. prod<u>u</u>ce   B. prod<u>u</u>ct   C. <u>u</u>nique   D. <u>u</u>niversity

( ) 2. <u>e</u>thnic   A. marv<u>e</u>lous   B. d<u>e</u>votion   C. tick<u>e</u>t   D. r<u>e</u>servation

( ) 3. s<u>ou</u>thern   A. thr<u>ou</u>ghout   B. d<u>ou</u>ble   C. d<u>ou</u>bt   D. marvel<u>ou</u>s

( ) 4. produ<u>c</u>t   A. dis<u>c</u>over   B. agen<u>c</u>y   C. experien<u>c</u>e   D. <u>c</u>ity

( ) 5. <u>a</u>void   A. <u>a</u>gency   B. n<u>a</u>tion   C. n<u>a</u>tional   D. wom<u>a</u>n

二、英汉互译

1. all sorts of _____
2. 因……著名_____
3. 放弃_____
4. be worth doing _____
5. take care of _____
6. be rich in _____
7. scenic spot _____
8. 穿过；通过_____
9. 出发_____
10. 因为；应归于_____

三、用括号内所给汉语提示或单词的适当形式填空

1. Li Siguang is one of the most famous _____（地理学家）in China.

2. He _____（give）up his studies and went on the stage.

3. We _____（发现）that our luggage had been stolen.

4. He _____（经历了）all sorts of difficulties and hardships, when he was young.

5. Xu Xiake spent over 30 years travelling _____（遍及）the country.

6. The diary _____（最终）became *The Travel Notes of Xu Xiake*.

7. In his youth, he showed great _____（兴趣）in travel and began his trips.

8. The students crowed into the hall, shouting _____（exciting）.

9. Although he experienced all sorts of hardships, Xu Xiake never thought of _____（quit）.

10. He avoided _____（comfort）travel options and chose to go almost everywhere on foot.

四、找出下列句子中错误的选项，并改正过来

1. He <u>spent</u> <u>over</u> 2 hours <u>to finished</u> <u>doing</u> his homework.
       A   B   C   D

2. <u>Although</u> he experienced <u>all sorts of</u> difficulties, Xu never <u>thought of</u> <u>quit</u>.
     A   B   C   D

3. She <u>went</u> <u>to bed</u> <u>until</u> she finished <u>doing</u> her housework.
        A   B   C   D

4. Why <u>don't</u> <u>you</u> <u>to ask</u> your friend <u>to help</u> you?
          A   B   C   D

5. <u>This kind of</u> <u>computer</u> <u>is</u> three <u>thousands</u> yuan.
        A   B   C   D

1.(　　)应为_____　　2.(　　)应为_____　　3.(　　)应为_____

4.(　　)应为_____　　5.(　　)应为_____

单元检测

第一部分　英语知识运用(共分三节，满分40分)

第一节　语音知识：从 A、B、C、D 四个选项中找出其画线部分与所给单词画线部分读音相同的选项。(共5分，每小题1分)

(　　)1. thr<u>ou</u>ghout　　A. th<u>ou</u>gh　　B. t<u>o</u>gether　　C. <u>e</u>thnic　　D. th<u>o</u>se

(　　)2. c<u>o</u>ver　　A. l<u>o</u>cal　　B. <u>o</u>ption　　C. m<u>o</u>ney　　D. dev<u>o</u>tion

(　　)3. s<u>ou</u>th　　A. thr<u>ou</u>ghout　　B. d<u>ou</u>ble　　C. s<u>ou</u>thern　　D. marvel<u>ou</u>s

(　　)4. quest<u>io</u>n　　A. <u>o</u>ption　　B. reservat<u>io</u>n　　C. vegetat<u>io</u>n　　D. suggest<u>io</u>n

(　　)5. pr<u>o</u>duce　　A. disc<u>o</u>ver　　B. agency　　C. <u>o</u>cean　　D. c<u>o</u>llege

第二节　词汇与语法知识：从 A、B、C、D 四个选项中选出可以填入空白处的最佳选项。(共25分，每小题1分)

(　　)6. Xu Xiake became interested in books about different places at _____ early age.

        A. a　　　　B. an　　　　C. /　　　　D. the

(　　)7. There are _____ famous scenic spots here.

    A. a great many of　　　　　　　　B. a great many

    C. a great deal　　　　　　　　　　D. a great deal of

( )8. Shangri-La _____ the Pudacuo National Park.
   A. is famous to   B. is famous as
   C. is famous for   D. famous for

( )9. This place is really worth _____.
   A. visiting   B. to visiting   C. to visit   D. for visiting

( )10. _____ his devotion, the diary eventually became *The Travel Notes of Xu Xiake*.
   A. Because   B. Though   C. Thanks for   D. Due to

( )11. Although he experienced all sorts of difficulties and hardships, _____ he never thought of quitting.
   A. but   B. because   C. /   D. since

( )12. When did you _____ Beijing?
   A. arrive   B. reach   C. got to   D. reached

( )13. I'm _____ in this story. Can you tell it again?
   A. interested   B. interest   C. interesting   D. interests

( )14. I enjoyed _____ music when I was young.
   A. listened to   B. listened   C. listening to   D. listening

( )15. Could you _____ the old things in the past?
   A. think of   B. think about   C. think over   D. think

( )16. Her dream _____ China has come true at last with the help of her grandfather.
   A. to visit   B. in visiting   C. visiting   D. of visiting

( )17. He tried to avoid _____ my questions.
   A. answering   B. to answering   C. to answer   D. answer

( )18. Since we didn't _____ the firework, the environment in my hometown has become better and better.
   A. set out   B. set about   C. set off   D. set up

( )19. English is not easy, but I never _____.
   A. give up it   B. give it up   C. take it up   D. show it off

( )20. _____ Mrs Zhang, we could get to school on time.
   A. Thanks for   B. Thanks to
   C. Thank you for   D. Thank you to

( )21. Look up and you can see _____ stars in the sky at night.
   A. million   B. three millions

    C. million of   D. millions of

( )22. It _____ me 2 hours _____ for the information about the space.
   A. taken; searching   B. cost; to search
   C. cost; searching   D. took; to search

( )23. —How was your weekend?
   —Very good. I _____ the science museum with my classmates.
   A. visited   B. visit   C. am visiting   D. will visit

( )24. Sara _____ a new song. I practiced _____ it.
   A. writes; sing   B. writes; singing
   C. wrote; sing   D. wrote; singing

( )25. *Black Beauty* is _____ a sad story that it _____ me when I read it last week.
   A. such; touches   B. such; touched
   C. so; touch   D. so; touching

( )26. She _____ to bed until she finished _____ her homework.
   A. went; to do   B. went; doing
   C. didn't go; to do   D. didn't go; doing

( )27. The Great Wall is one of the man-made _____ of the world.
   A. wonders   B. sight   C. view   D. wonder

( )28. He is poor in money, but rich in _____.
   A. knowledge   B. communications   C. attention   D. business

( )29. —Do you have _____ about what to do for the May Day holiday, Millie?
   —Yes. I'm planning to _____.
   A. any ideas; travel to abroad
   B. some ideas; travel abroad
   C. some ideas; travel to abroad
   D. any ideas; travel abroad

( )30. We didn't know how to find them because they didn't tell us _____.
   A. which room did they live
   B. which room they lived in
   C. which room they lived
   D. which room did they live in

第三节 完形填空：阅读下面的短文，从所给的 A、B、C、D 四个选项中选出正确的答案。(共 10 分，每小题 1 分)

In America, cars are very popular. When the kids are fourteen years old, they dream __31__ having their own __32__. Many students work after school to buy a car. In most places young people learn to __33__ in high school. They have to take a driving test to get a __34__. Learning to drive and getting a driver's license may be one of the most exciting things in their lives. For many, that piece of __35__ is an important symbol that they are now grown-ups.

Americans seem to love their cars almost more than anything else. People almost never go to see a __36__ when they are sick. But they will take their cars to a "__37__" at the smallest sign of a problem. At weekends, people spend most of the time __38__ washing and waxing(打蜡) their cars. For some families it is not enough to have __39__ car. They often have two or even three. Husbands need a car to go to work. Housewives need a car to go shopping or to take the children to school or __40__ activities.

( )31. A. of   B. at   C. on   D. to
( )32. A. computers   B. cars   C. bikes   D. houses
( )33. A. ride   B. play   C. cook   D. drive
( )34. A. book   B. address   C. licence   D. passport
( )35. A. address   B. passport   C. book   D. paper
( )36. A. doctor   B. nurse   C. teacher   D. professor
( )37. A. shop   B. factory   C. university   D. hospital
( )38. A. at   B. on   C. in   D. with
( )39. A. no   B. one   C. some   D. several
( )40. A. other   B. another   C. others   D. else

第二部分　篇章与词汇理解(共分三节，满分 50 分)

第一节　阅读理解：阅读下列短文，从每题所给的 A、B、C、D 四个选项中，选出最恰当的答案。(共 30 分，每小题 2 分)

A

My father decided to take me on a trip to France when I was 15 years old. I had never been out of the country before, so I was very excited. My aunt, my father and I went around with my father showing us all the unbelievable sites in Paris. None of us spoke much French but we loved the city.

Unit 1 Travel

We had taken the subway all over the city and were congratulating ourselves on our mastering what is honestly a brilliant subway design that is pretty easy to follow. We decided to visit Versailles by train. We chatted happily along the way until my father realized we were far into the French countryside and no one around spoke English. We reached the end of the line and felt frightened when everyone finally left the train. An old man and his grandchild noticed us and came to help. He spoke no English, so in broken French we tried to explain. When he finally understood, this great man settled his grandson and showed us to the correct train and then boarded with us.

Later we knew the truth that there was a train transfer and he didn't want us to miss it. This kind man rode a train for an hour and a half out of his way to make sure that three Americans got where they wanted to be. He refused to let us pay for his ticket. He did it all with a gentle smile and patted our hands gently at the stop. Then in his quiet way, he boarded the train to return the way he had come.

What impressed me most was the man and his kindness during the amazing trip. Some Americans think the French are rude for some reason, but I always try to persuade them to change their minds with this story.

( )41. At 15 years old, the author' family took a trip to _____?

  A. France B. subway C. Versailles D. unbelievable sites

( )42. What happened to the author and his family on the train?

  A. They failed to get off the train at the right time.

  B. They couldn't understand the signs of the train.

  C. They had a quarrel about where to go first.

  D. They found it hard to live in the countryside.

( )43. How did the man help the author and his family?

  A. By paying for their train tickets.

  B. By showing them the return way.

  C. By inviting them to travel together.

  D. By leading them to their place.

( )44. Which of the following can best describe the last paragraph?

  A. Seeing is believing.

  B. Being kind is a good manner.

  C. Traveling enriches one's life.

  D. Helping brings great pleasure.

(   )45. What's the purpose of the author's writing the passage?

A. To explain an unexpected problem.

B. To list the unbelievable sites in Paris.

C. To share an unforgettable foreign experience.

D. To show the importance of mastering a foreign language.

B

Different countries have different customs. When you travel to another countries, please follow their customs, just as the saying goes, "_____."

Very often people who travel to the United States forget to tip. It is usual to tip porters who help carry your bags, taxi drivers and waiters. Waiters expect to get a 15% tip on the cost of your meal. Taxi drivers expect about the same amount.

In England, make sure to stand in line even if there are only two of you. It's important to respect lines there. It's a good idea to talk about the weather. It's a favorite subject of conversation with the British.

In Spain, it's a good idea to have a light meal in the afternoon if someone invites you for dinner. People have dinner very late, and restaurants do not generally open until after 9 pm.

In Arab countries, men kiss one another on the cheek. Your host may welcome you with a kiss on both cheeks. It is polite for you to do the same.

In Japan, people usually give personal or business cards to each other when they meet for the first time. When a person gives you a card, don't put it into your pocket right away. The person expects you to read it.

Don't forget to be careful of your body language to express something in conversation. A kind of body language that is acceptable in one culture may be impolite in another.

(   )46. When you travel to the USA, you don't need to tip _____.

A. porters   B. waiters   C. taxi drivers   D. conductor

(   )47. The missing sentence in the first paragraph should be"_____."

A. Love me, love my dog

B. He who laughs last laughs best

C. When in Rome, do as the Romans do

D. Where there is a will, there is a way

(   )48. The underline word "porters" in the passage means _____.

A. 搬运工   B. 清洁工   C. 接线员   D. 售票员

(　　)49. Which of the following is TRUE according to the passage?

　　A. In Spain, People usually have dinner very early.

　　B. In England it's a not polite to talk about the weather.

　　C. In Arab countries, men kiss one another on the cheek.

　　D. In Japan you should not read the business card as soon as you get it.

(　　)50. What's the best title of the passage?

　　A. How to Tip.　　　　　　　B. Body Language.

　　C. When to Have Dinner.　　D. Advice to International Travelers.

C

More and more people like bicycling and it is no surprise. It is fun, healthy and good for the environment. Maybe that's why there are 1.4 billion bicycles and only 400 million cars on roads worldwide today. Bikes can take you almost anywhere, and there is no oil cost!

Get on a bicycle and ride around your neighbourhood. You may discover something new all around you. Stopping and getting off a bike is easier than stopping and getting out of your car. You can bike to work and benefit from the enjoyable exercise without polluting the environment. You don't even have to ride all the way.

Folding bikes work well for people who ride the train. Just fold the bike and take it with you. You can do the same on an airplane. A folding bike can be packed in a suitcase. You can also take a common bike with you when you fly. But be sure to look for information by getting on airline websites. Not all airlines are bicycle-friendly to travellers.

Health Benefits of Bicycling:

It helps to prevent heart diseases.

Bicycling helps to control your weight.

A 15-minute bike ride to and from work three times a week burns off five kilos of fat in a year.

Bicycling can improve your mood.

Exercise like bicycling has been shown to make people feel better, more relaxed and self-confident.

Bicycling is healthier than driving.

(　　)51. From the passage, we know that bicycling is becoming very _____.

　　A. surprising　　B. exciting　　C. expensive　　D. popular

( )52. When you are riding your bicycle around your neighbourhood, you may _____.

　　A. pollute the environment around

　　B. find something you didn't notice

　　C. go everywhere and use a little oil

　　D. go off your bike and begin to work

( )53. If you travel with a folding bike, you can fold it and _____.

　　A. get out of the car　　　　B. take it onto a train

　　C. put it in your purse　　　D. go on airline websites

( )54. One of the benefits from bicycling is that _____.

　　A. you can fold the bicycle　　B. you will be friendly to others

　　C. you will be more relaxed　　D. you will get fatter and fatter

( )55. Which is TRUE according to the passage?

　　A. Bicycling is enjoyable exercise for people.

　　B. Driving cars is healthier than riding bikes.

　　C. Riding a bike pollutes your neighbourhood.

　　D. Common bikes are welcomed by all airlines.

第二节　词义搭配：从(B)栏中选出(A)栏单词的正确解释。(共10分，每小题1分)

　　　　　(A)　　　　　　　　　　(B)

( )56. unique　　　　　A. wonderful; extraordinarily good

( )57. reach　　　　　　B. the only one of its kind

( )58. eventually　　　　C. physically relaxed; pleasant

( )59. comfortable　　　D. a thing that is produced, usually for sale

( )60. marvelous　　　　E. to arrive at/in

( )61. reservation　　　F. finally

( )62. hardship　　　　G. an arrangement; booking

( )63. major　　　　　H. a situation that is difficult and unpleasant

( )64. journey　　　　I. the act of traveling from one place to another

( )65. product　　　　J. very large or important

第三节　补全对话：根据对话内容，从对话后的选项中选出能填入空白处的最佳选项。(共10分，每小题2分)

A: Excuse me, can you do me a favor?

B: Yes, of course. ___66___.

A: __67__

B: When and where did you last use it?

A: I made a call to my friend when I left my room for lunch, and then I came back to find it lost.

B: __68__.

A: OK. I hope it will be found quickly. You know, I'm really worried about it.

B: __69__ Once we get the news, we'll inform you as soon as possible. Please don't worry. __70__.

A: Yes. George, Room 222, sorry to trouble you.

B: You're welcome.

> A. I'll call the Lost and Found Department immediately.
> B. May I have your name and room number?
> C. What's the matter with you, sir?
> D. All right. We'll try our best to find it.
> E. I can't find my mobile phone.

第三部分 语言技能应用(共分四节,满分30分)

第一节 单词拼写:根据下列句子及所给汉语注释,在相应题号后的横线上写出该单词的正确形式。(共5分,每小题1分)

71. Qian Xuesen's _____(付出) to China was expressed in his saying. "My career is in China."

72. The Great Pyramid was considered a _____(独特的) building in the 19th century.

73. He checked his homework carefully to _____(避免) making mistakes.

74. His interest in law led him _____(最终) to become a lawyer.

75. Why not visit our _____(当地的) theaters with us?

第二节 词形变换:用括号内单词的适当形式填空。(共5分,每小题1分)

76. He lived in a room with an air-conditioner _____(comfortable).

77. I'm going to get some brochures from the travel _____(agency).

78. I think the Great Wall is worth _____(visit).

79. He spent over 41 years _____(travel) throughout the world.

80. In his youth, he was _____(interest) in geography.

第三节 改错：从 A、B、C、D 四个画线处找出一处错误的选项，填入括号内，并在横线上写出正确答案。(共 10 分，每小题 2 分)

81. What was he do when I was not at home last weekend.
　　　A　　B　　　　　C　　　D

82. The Smiths arrived Beijing and visited the Great Wall.
　　　　A　　　B　　　　　　C　　D

83. He finished his homework without make any mistakes.
　　　　A　　　B　　　　　　C　　D

84. The cars made in this city are more expensive than that made in that city.
　　　　　A　　　　　　B　　　　　C　　　D

85. Help you to some fruit, girls.
　　　A　B　C　　D

81.(　　)应为_____ 82.(　　)应为_____ 83.(　　)应为_____
84.(　　)应为_____ 85.(　　)应为_____

第四节 书面表达。(共 10 分)

作文题目：Travelling

词数要求：80~100 词

写作要点：1. 旅行受到越来越多的人喜爱；
　　　　　2. 你对旅行的看法。

Unit 2

Health and Fitness

Warming-up

一、句型汇总

1. What's wrong with you? / What's the matter with you? 你怎么了?

2. I have a sore throat and a terrible cough. 我喉咙疼,咳嗽得厉害。

3. I am afraid you have a bad cold. 恐怕你患了重感冒。

4. Is there anything I can do about it? 对此我能做些什么吗?

5. There are washing machines to wash our clothes. 有洗衣机洗我们的衣服。

6. Most of us have jobs that involve little physical effort. 我们大多数人的工作几乎不需要体力。

7. If exercise were a pill, it would be one of the best medicines ever invented. 如果锻炼是一种药丸,它将是其中最好的发明之一。

8. Even though it comes from Chinese culture, I believe it can have a benefit to any other culture. 尽管它来自中国文化,但我相信它对任何其他文化都有好处。

二、英汉互译

1. stomachache _____   2. under pressure _____

3. allergy _____   4. have a sore throat _____
5. lose our temper _____   6. 看病_____
7. 大量的水_____   8. 好好休息一下_____
9. 感觉疲劳_____   10. 向别人寻求帮助_____

Listening and Speaking

一、找出与所给单词画线部分读音相同的选项

( )1. tech<u>n</u>ician   A. temperature   B. re<u>m</u>ind   C. recover   D. re<u>m</u>ember
( )2. <u>a</u>ppointment   A. <u>a</u>ctive B. <u>a</u>ctually C. <u>a</u>ttention D. <u>a</u>ncient
( )3. rec<u>o</u>ver   A. thr<u>oa</u>t B. l<u>o</u>cal   C. dev<u>o</u>tion D. m<u>o</u>nth
( )4. st<u>o</u>machache   A. sch<u>oo</u>l B. w<u>a</u>tch   C. ch<u>oo</u>se   D. ch<u>a</u>llenge
( )5. heal<u>th</u>y   A. dream   B. brea<u>th</u>   C. repea<u>t</u>   D. meaning

二、从(B)栏中找出与(A)栏中相对应的答语

(A)

1. What's wrong with you?
2. Is there anything I can do about it?
3. What else should I pay attention to?
4. When can I recover from it?
5. How long have you been like this?

(B)

A. Yes, there is, take this medicine one tablet there times a day.
B. I have a bad cold.
C. You should do more exercises.
D. Since yesterday morning.
E. It will take about two weeks.

三、用所给句子补全下面对话

A: Morning! 1

B: I've got a sore throat and a headache.

A: Do you feel tired?

B: Yes, my whole body feels weak. 2

A: I'm sorry to hear that. I'll have to examine you. Open your mouth wide so that I can look at your throat. Yes, It's very red. I'll have to give you an injection.

B: 3

A：An injection is better than pills.

B：Are you sure? 4

A：But you'd better have an injection first. It is more helpful.

B：OK. 5

A：Probably, if you take a rest today.

B：I will have a good rest today so that I'll be able to go out tomorrow.

> A. Will I be able to go out tomorrow?
> B. I really feel terrible.
> C. Can you give me some pills?
> D. I hate injections.
> E. What's wrong with you, madam?

四、场景模拟

编写一组对话,昨天晚上你感觉身体不舒服,早上去看医生。

提示词汇：feel tired; take one's temperature; stay up late; drink plenty of water; don't worry; relax yourself; have a good rest; take some medicine

_____
_____
_____
_____
_____
_____

Reading and Writing

一、用括号内所给汉语提示或单词的适当形式填空

1. She takes an _____ (活跃的) part in school sports every year.

2. He died of lung _____ (癌症) last year.

3. Time is a _____ (有价值的) resource.

4. Physical activity can also boost _____ (自尊心) and mood.

5. There are _____ (wash) machines to wash our clothes.

6. _____ (burn) coal is one of the causes of the air pollution.

7. With the _____ (develop) of science and technology, China is becoming more and more powerful.

8. _____ (tradition) Chinese medicine has a history of several years.

9. What color is our _____ (nation) flag?

10. The handsome young man is always _____ (confidence) with himself.

二、完形填空

Throughout Chinese history. Traditional Chinese Medicine (TCM) played an important role __1__ health. Developed over the course of more than five __2__ years, TCM is unique __3__ its special method of treatment, including acupuncture（针灸）and medical massage. Chinese medicine is based __4__ the theory of yin and yang and the five elements. __5__ by these theories, doctors of TCM emphasize __6__ localized treatment but also treatment of the body as a whole. Doctors use four basic diagnostic methods: observing, listening and smelling, inquiring and __7__ with hands. Of all the methods pulse feeling is __8__ important.

Thanks __9__ TCM, millions of lives in the country __10__ saved in the past year. And it is becoming more and more popular in the world.

( ) 1. A. in   B. on   C. a   D. /
( ) 2. A. thousands   B. thousands of   C. thousand   D. thousand of
( ) 3. A. because   B. because of   C. with   D. cause of
( ) 4. A. in   B. to   C. of   D. on
( ) 5. A. Guiding   B. To guide   C. Guided   D. Guide
( ) 6. A. not   B. only   C. not only   D. no only
( ) 7. A. tasting   B. smelling   C. looking   D. feeling
( ) 8. A. more   B. most   C. the most   D. the more
( ) 9. A. to   B. of   C. for   D. with
( ) 10. A. were   B. have been   C. has been   D. are

三、阅读理解

阅读下面短文，从每题所给的 A、B、C、D 四个选项中选出最佳答案。

Mrs. White was having a lot of trouble with her skin, so she went to her doctor about it. He could not find anything wrong with her, so he sent her to the local hospital for tests. The hospital, of course, sent the results of the tests directly to Mrs. White's doctor, and the next morning he telephoned her to give her a list of things that he thought she should not eat, as any of them might be the cause of her skin trouble.

Mrs. White carefully wrote all the things down on a piece of paper, which she then left beside the telephone while she went out to a ladies' meeting.

When she got back home two hours later, she found her husband waiting for her. He had a big basket full of packages beside him, and when he saw her, he said, "Hello, dear. I have done all your shopping for you."

"Done all my shopping?" she asked in surprise. "But how did you know what I wanted?"

Well. When I got home, I found your shopping list beside the telephone, " answered her husband." So I went down to the shops and bought everything you had written down.

(　　) 1. Mrs. White's doctor sent her to the local hospital because _____.
   A. Mrs. White was having a lot of trouble with her skin
   B. Mrs. White wanted him to do so
   C. the doctor couldn't tell her what was wrong with her
   D. the doctor wanted to please Miss White

(　　) 2. Mrs. White's doctor phoned her and told her _____.
   A. to go to his clinic the next morning
   B. to go to the ladies' meeting
   C. to write some things down on a piece of paper
   D. a list of things she should not eat

(　　) 3. When Mrs. White got back home, she saw a basket full of packages which were _____.
   A. bought by her husband
   B. sent to her by some of her friends
   C. delivered by the shops
   D. given to her by her doctor

(　　) 4. Mr. White bought _____.
   A. what his wife liked most
   B. just what his wife should not eat
   C. the things his wife had asked him to buy
   D. the things his wife didn't want to eat

(　　) 5. Which of the following could be the best title for the passage?
   A. Shopping List.　　　　　　　　B. Mrs. White and Her Husband.
   C. Doing Shopping.　　　　　　　D. What a Husband.

四、书面表达

作文题目:以"How to keep healthy"为题,写一篇文章,词数:80~100词。

写作要求:

1. 做好个人防护,每天戴口罩,常洗手,勤换衣服等;

2. 保持良好的饮食和生活习惯,多吃水果、蔬菜,不吃垃圾食品;

3. 进行户外运动,适当体育锻炼。

Grammar

一、从下面每小题四个选项中选出最佳选项

( ) 1. There is a lot of work _____ .

  A. do   B. done   C. to be done   D. to do

( ) 2. There is nothing in the handbag, _____ ?

  A. isn't it   B. is it   C. isn't there   D. is there

( ) 3. Traveling is _____ . But people may often feel _____ when they are back from travels.

  A. excite; tiring   B. exciting; tired

  C. excited; tired   D. exciting; tiring

( ) 4. When spring comes, the weather gets _____ .

  A. warm and warm   B. warmer and warmer

  C. warmer or warmer   D. warm or warm

( ) 5. When you visit a museum, you should _____ rules and don't be against them.

  A. compare with   B. look forward to

  C. pay attention to   D. come up with

Unit 2 Health and Fitness

(　　)6. There is _____ with my computer.
　　A. wrong something　　　　　　B. something wrong
　　C. anything wrong　　　　　　　D. wrong anything

(　　)7. She is _____ honest girl and is studying in _____ university.
　　A. a; an　　　B. the; an　　　C. /; a　　　D. an; a

(　　)8. In fact, it is not good _____ your health _____ eat much fast food.
　　A. for; to　　　B. to; to　　　C. to; for　　　D. for; for

(　　)9. There _____ a football match next week in our school.
　　A. is　　　B. are　　　C. will be　　　D. have

(　　)10. My sister _____ the cold very quickly.
　　A. recovered　　B. recover　　C. recovered from　　D. recovering from

(　　)11. There is little milk in the bottle, _____?
　　A. isn't there　　B. is there　　C. there is　　D. are there

(　　)12. There _____ some water in the glass.
　　A. are　　　B. aren't　　　C. is　　　D. be

(　　)13. The water _____ cool when I jumped into the swimming pool for morning exercise.
　　A. was felt　　B. is felt　　C. felt　　D. feels

(　　)14. As you can see, the number of cars on the road _____ rising these days.
　　A. was keeping　　B. keep　　C. keeps　　D. were

(　　)15. Tom sounds very much _____ in the job, but I'm not sure whether he can manage it.
　　A. interested　　B. interesting　　C. interestingly　　D. interestedly

(　　)16. This kind of fruit _____ very sweet.
　　A. looks　　　B. feels　　　C. tastes　　　D. sounds

(　　)17. The three of us _____ around China for about two months last year.
　　A. travelled　　B. have travelled　　C. had travelled　　D. travel

(　　)18. My brother _____ hard for long to realize his dream.
　　A. works　　B. is working　　C. has worked　　D. worked

(　　)19. When he called me last night, I _____ TV.
　　A. was watching　　B. is watching　　C. have watched　　D. have had

(　　)20. E-mail, as well as mobiles phones _____ an important part in our life.
　　A. is playing　　B. have played　　C. are playing　　D. play

( )21. There _____ a number of people in the park.
　　　　A. is　　　　B. be　　　　C. are　　　　D. was

( )22. It is _____ that all the people like it.
　　　　A. so excited a movie　　　　B. such a exciting movie
　　　　C. so exciting a movie　　　　D. such an excited movie

( )23. By next month he _____ in the city for five years.
　　　　A. has worked　　　　B. has been working
　　　　C. work　　　　D. will have worked

( )24. I don't feel _____ today.
　　　　A. good　　　B. well　　　C. nice　　　D. better

( )25. I _____ travelling very much. In 2008, I _____ to Guilin and next year I _____ to the USA.
　　　　A. like; go; went　　　　B. likes; went; go
　　　　C. like; went; will go　　　　D. like; go; will go.

( )26. My brother _____ up early every day.
　　　　A. gets used to get　　　　B. is used to getting
　　　　C. is used to get　　　　D. used to getting

( )27. We _____ for my father in the shop now.
　　　　A. are waiting　　B. wait　　C. waited　　D. waits

( )28. —Your grandmother has _____ been to the Summer Palace before, has she?
　　—_____
　　　　A. never; No, he has　　　　B. ever; No, she hasn't
　　　　C. already; Yes, she hasn't　　　　D. never; No, she hasn't

( )29. A number of students _____ in the library and the number of them _____ 89.
　　　　A. were; were　　　　B. was; were
　　　　C. were; was　　　　D. was; was

( )30. we should not _____ our _____ even if we are very angry.
　　　　A. lose, temper　　　　B. control, temper
　　　　C. lose, tempers　　　　D. control, tempers

二、找出下列句子中错误的选项,并改正过来

1. There has about twenty stores in this town.
　　A　　B　　C　　　　　　D

2. There are a pen and three books on the table.
        A   B   C   D

3. We are always in a bad mood in Friday.
            A   B   C D

4. The Greens has been in China for five years.
   A   B   C   D

5. I saw a thief stolen a wallet and I called 110 at once.
     A   B   C   D

6. There is a lot of homework to do this week.
         A   B   C   D

7. We ignored it for too long.
      A   B C   D

8. You get over the cold in a week.
       A   B   C   D

9. Smoking does great harmful to our health.
      A   B   C   D

10. Learn English is difficult but interesting.
       A   B   C   D

1.(　　)应为_____   2.(　　)应为_____   3.(　　)应为_____
4.(　　)应为_____   5.(　　)应为_____   6.(　　)应为_____
7.(　　)应为_____   8.(　　)应为_____   9.(　　)应为_____
10.(　　)应为_____

For Better Performance

一、找出与所给单词画线部分读音相同的选项

(　　) 1. sugge<u>st</u>ion   A. que<u>st</u>ion   B. popula<u>t</u>ion   C. a<u>t</u>tention   D. reserva<u>t</u>ion

(　　) 2. heal<u>th</u>   A. ra<u>th</u>er   B. wea<u>th</u>er   C. brea<u>th</u>   D. al<u>th</u>ough

(　　) 3. c<u>a</u>ncer   A. <u>a</u>gency   B. m<u>a</u>jor   C. <u>a</u>ctive   D. <u>a</u>round

(　　) 4. <u>e</u>nergy   A. v<u>e</u>getation B. gu<u>e</u>st   C. program   D. hungry

(　　) 5. te<u>ch</u>nology   A. spee<u>ch</u>   B. stoma<u>ch</u>   C. <u>ch</u>oice   D. <u>ch</u>allenge

二、英汉互译

1. public transport _____   2. as a result _____

3. give sb a hand _____   4. washing machine _____

5. move around _____   6. 燃尽；烧掉 _____

7. 发脾气_____ 8. 而且_____
9. 忍受；遭受_____ 10. 恢复_____

三、用括号内所给汉语提示或单词的适当形式填空

1. I have to make an _____ (appoint) to get braces for my teeth.

2. There are many _____ (tradition) activities during the Spring Festival.

3. You can have a good _____ (communicate) with him if you have different opinions.

4. Life is difficult. This is one of the greatest _____ (true).

5. Good habits are good for the _____ (develop) of us teenagers.

6. Thank you for your _____ (value) help and practical advice.

7. _____ (physics) activity can also boost self-respect and mood.

8. What school _____ (active) do you often participate in.

9. As an _____ (experience) teacher, you should help the young teachers to improve their teaching methods and skills.

10. Many people want to live a _____ (health) life now.

四、找出下列句子中错误的选项,并改正过来

1. I'm more busier today than yesterday.
      A   B   C   D

2. If you keep healthy, you should avoid to eat too much fat and sugar.
          A   B   C   D

3. He is used to live a simple life.
      A B   C   D

4. I like this silk dress because it is felt so soft and comfortable.
      A   B   C   D

5. It took us two hours finished the task.
       A B   C   D

1.(　　)应为_____ 2.(　　)应为_____ 3.(　　)应为_____
4.(　　)应为_____ 5.(　　)应为_____

Unit 2　Health and Fitness

单元检测

第一部分　英语知识运用(共分三节，满分40分)

第一节　语音知识：从A、B、C、D四个选项中找出其画线部分与所给单词画线部分读音相同的选项。(共5分，每小题1分)

(　　)1. tooth<u>a</u>che　　A. stom<u>a</u>ch　　B. ch<u>oi</u>ce　　C. ch<u>a</u>llenge　　D. sp<u>ee</u>ch

(　　)2. s<u>u</u>ffer　　A. tr<u>u</u>e　　B. s<u>u</u>cceed　　C. l<u>u</u>ggage　　D. <u>u</u>nique

(　　)3. <u>e</u>nergy　　A. r<u>e</u>duce　　B. r<u>e</u>cover　　C. <u>e</u>ffort　　D. d<u>e</u>votion

(　　)4. c<u>ou</u>gh　　A. th<u>ou</u>ght　　B. d<u>ou</u>ble　　C. tr<u>ou</u>ble　　D. pr<u>ou</u>d

(　　)5. b<u>oo</u>st　　A. c<u>oo</u>k　　B. f<u>oo</u>d　　C. mushr<u>oo</u>m　　D. l<u>oo</u>k

第二节　词汇与语法知识：从A、B、C、D四个选项中选出可以填入空白处的最佳选项。(共25分，每小题1分)

(　　)6. Miss Wang is ill. Her daughter is looking after her in the hospital. _____

　　A. I'm sorry to hear that.　　B. Not at all.

　　C. I'm afraid not.　　D. It doesn't matter.

(　　)7. —I'd like to make an appointment with your manager tomorrow.

　　—_____.

　　A. No. you mustn't

　　B. Try again tomorrow afternoon

　　C. I'm sorry, but he is engaged tomorrow afternoon

　　D. Thanks for calling me

(　　)8. Is there _____ in today's newspaper?

　　A. special something　　B. nothing special

　　C. anything special　　D. special anything

(　　)9. I could keep my temper even if I were very angry. Which of the following phrases can replace the one underlined?

　　—_____.

　　A. lose my temper　　B. control my temper

　　C. Lose one's temper　　D. control one's temper

31

( )10. The _____ doctor is a doctor with a lot of _____. Yesterday, he talked about his _____ during his stay in the hospital.

    A. experienced; experience; experiences

    B. experienced; experiencing; experience

    C. experiencing; experienced; experiences

    D. experienced; experience; experiencing

( )11. Many people think that smoking makes them _____ happy and _____ them relax.

    A. feel; helps   B. feels; helps

    C. to feel; help   D. feel; help

( )12. Thank you for all your hard work last week. I don't think we _____ it without you.

    A. can manage   B. could have managed

    C. could manage   D. can have managed

( )13. Eating vegetables can keep our bodies _____.

    A. health   B. healthy   C. healthier   D. more healthy

( )14. Reading _____ an important role _____ learning English.

    A. play; in   B. plays; in   C. take; in   D. takes; in

( )15. Watching too much computer _____ many bad effects _____ our eyes.

    A. have; on   B. have; to   C. has; on   D. has; to

( )16. You'd better give up smoking, if you want to stay _____.

    A. healthy   B. unhealthy   C. health   D. healthier

( )17. You'd better _____ tomorrow morning.

    A. to have cut your hair   B. have your hair cutted

    C. have your hair cut   D. had cut your hair

( )18. We _____ all the dead leaves in the garden yesterday.

    A. burned off   B. burned with

    C. burned to   D. burned on

( )19. The police _____ catching the thief _____ stole the car.

    A. is; who   B. are; who   C. are; whom   D. is; whom

( )20. We will go to have a picnic if it _____ tomorrow.

    A. don't rain   B. doesn't rain

    C. didn't rain   D. rain

(   )21. We won't give up _____ we should fail ten times.
  A. if　　　　B. as if　　　　C. as long as　　　　D. even though

(   )22. In fact, it is not good _____ your health _____ eat much fast food.
  A. for; to　　B. to; to　　C. to; for　　D. for; for

(   )23. Mike has been working hard day and night for months. _____, he is sick now.
  A. In return　　　　　　　B. As a result
  C. In a way　　　　　　　D. As well

(   )24. The doctor advised him to give up _____, but he refused _____ so.
  A. to smoke; doing　　　　B. smoking; to do
  C. to smoke; to do　　　　D. smoking; doing

(   )25. He appears to be strong and healthy, but _____ he suffers from a very weak heart.
  A. as a matter of fact　　B. what's more
  C. accordingly　　　　　　D. no wonder

(   )26. Nowadays people begin to pay _____ to their daily diet.
  A. notice　　B. attention　　C. a look　　D. thought

(   )27. If we work with a strong will, we can overcome any difficulty, _____ great it is.
  A. what　　B. how　　C. however　　D. whatever

(   )28. Jim studies harder than _____ in his class.
  A. any students　　　　　B. any other student
  C. any student　　　　　　D. the student

(   )29. If I _____ you, I would take part in the ball game.
  A. were　　B. are　　C. be　　D. was

(   )30. He did not attend the meeting because he had caught _____.
  A. heavy cold　　　　　　B. heavy a cold
  C. the heavy cold　　　　D. a heavy cold

第三节　完形填空：阅读下面的短文，从所给的A、B、C、D四个选项中选出正确的答案。(共10分，每小题1分)

Dear angels in white,

　　Hello! Today I say to you with great ___31___, you have worked hard.

　　The new coronavirus (冠状病毒), which ___32___ arrived, incited (煽动) the wings of death and wanted to take people ___33___ one by one. ___34___, as soon as the people were taken away by him, one by one angel in white ___35___, and now it is the New Year's holiday, but the angels in white still stand in their jobs, regardless of the day and night __36__ work. I saw on TV that some of them went to Wuhan despite the opposition of their families. Some of their children were still very young, and some doctors fell ill on the front line. Seeing these, my tears have __37__. __38__ valuable their spirit is! I'm going to learn from them. We firmly believe that __39__ we all have a heart that will never change, one life after another __40__.

They fought in the front line, risking their lives, in return. I love you! To the beloved angel in white!

(　　)31. A. admire　　　　B. to admire　　　　C. admiration　　　　D. admired
(　　)32. A. quietly　　　　B. quiet　　　　　　C. quite　　　　　　D. quitely
(　　)33. A. away　　　　　B. to　　　　　　　　C. for　　　　　　　D. out
(　　)34. A. But　　　　　　B. However　　　　　C. Therefore　　　　D. And
(　　)35. A. appear　　　　B. appearing　　　　C. appeared　　　　　D. to appear
(　　)36. A. overlook　　　B. overcome　　　　　C. overdo　　　　　　D. overload
(　　)37. A. come back　　 B. come about　　　　C. come away　　　　 D. come out
(　　)38. A. How　　　　　　B. What　　　　　　　C. How a　　　　　　 D. What a
(　　)39. A. as soon as　　B. as much as　　　　C. as long as　　　　D. as soon as possible
(　　)40. A. will save　　 B. will be saved　　 C. saved　　　　　　 D. is saved

第二部分　篇章与词汇理解(共分三节，满分50分)

第一节　阅读理解：阅读下列短文，从每题所给的A、B、C、D四个选项中，选出最恰当的答案。(共30分，每小题2分)

A

Different from popular thoughts, colds are not caused by bad weather. Colds are caused by viruses(病毒) in the body, and you are better out on the snowy day than you are in a warm room, with your friends, who just may be passing the virus around. If you feel a chill(寒冷) when you are coming down with a cold, you are already sick. A chill is an early sign of the cold.

The virus can spread through air when a cold-sufferer(感冒患者) coughs or sneezes. Surprisingly, this is not the most usual way of spreading. Many studies have now shown that most colds are "caught" by hands. A cold-sufferer rubs her nose, so spreading the virus to her hand. Then a friend comes to visit her. They shake their hands. The friend then gets something to eat by hand, and several days later she catches a cold. Although some parents pick up their children's tissues(纸巾) and carefully throw them away. They fail to wash their hands. They'll catch the colds, too.

Cold viruses can also be spread by objects, for example, telephones, plates. The cold-sufferer as well as other members of the house, by washing their hands often, will stop viruses from spreading in a way.

( )41. Colds are caused by _____.
   A. bad weather   B. chill   C. viruses   D. your friends

( )42. The underlined word "spread" means "_____" in Chinese.
   A. 翻译   B. 传播   C. 传送   D. 传统

( )43. Which of the following sentences is TRUE in the passage?
   A. An early sign of the cold is viruses in the body.
   B. The virus can't spread through air.
   C. Objects can spread cold viruses, too.
   D. Few colds are "caught" by hands.

( )44. People catch colds easily because they _____.
   A. rub their noses
   B. shake their hands
   C. pick up their children's tissues
   D. can't often wash their hands

( )45. The passage mainly tells us that _____.
   A. washing hands is a way to keep us from catching colds
   B. colds are caused by bad weather
   C. the cold-sufferer shakes hands with her friends
   D. we should stay in a warm room on the snowy day

B

American doctors say that mothers who smoke before their babies are born may slow the growth of their babies' lungs. They say reduced lung growth could cause the babies to suffer breathing problems and lung disease later in life. Doctors in Boston, Massachusetts studied 1,100 children. The mothers of some of the children smoked, the other mothers did not. Doctors found that the lungs of the children whose mothers smoked were 8% less developed than the lungs of the children whose mothers did not smoke, and that the children whose mothers smoked developed 20% more cold and breathing disease than other children later in life.

Another recent study found that children had a greater chance of developing lung cancer if their mothers smoked. The study also showed that the danger of lung cancer increased only for sons and not for daughters, and that the father's smoking did not affected child's chance of developing lung cancer.

(   )46. Doctors in Boston studied 1,100 children to _____.

　　A. examine whether these children were healthy

　　B. find out whether their mother had smoked

　　C. find why these children suffered breathing problems

　　D. look into the effect mothers' smoking had on their children

(   )47. Whose baby would have breathing diseases?

　　A. Mother who smokes cigarettes after their baby are born.

　　B. Mother who smokes cigarettes before their baby are born.

　　C. Mother who don't smoke at all.

　　D. Mother whose mother smokes.

(   )48. According to the text, which of the following is true?

　　A. The lungs of the children whose mothers smoked were 8% less developed than those of other children.

　　B. Mothers who smoked did not reduce the growth of their children's lungs.

　　C. The children whose mothers hadn't smoked developed 20% more cold and breathing diseases than other children.

　　D. The lungs of the children whose mothers didn't smoke were 8% less developed than others.

(   )49. Suppose John's father was a heavy smoker, so was Mary's mother. According to this text, _____.

　　A. John is more likely to develop lung cancer

　　B. Mary is more likely to develop lung cancer

　　C. John and Mary have the same chance to develop lung cancer

　　D. Neither John nor Mary has the chance to develop lung cancer

(   )50. The text is to _____.

　　A. warn us of the danger of smoking before children

　　B. warn people with breathing problems not to smoke

　　C. warn us that mothers who smoke may affect their children's health

　　D. warn us that fathers who smoke may affect their children as mothers

C

　　Many of us don't pay much attention to the importance of eye care.

　　It is said that if you take care of your body, then you can surely be healthy. That is why our eyes should be given a lot of care. Natural eyes care should be put in a number one place.

　　There are several causes leading to poor eyesight like not enough food, genes(基因) and aging. Televisions, computers and reading are also the cause of having poor eye sight. If you happen to work in front of the computer, it is best to take a break every once in a while. Something dirty can cause redness and they will make you feel uncomfortable. It is bad for your eyes, too. If this happens, the best way is to clean your eyes by using cold water. You must also try your best to protect your eyes from harmful things. For example, sunglasses are not just for fashion but they can also serve as a great way to protect your eyesight from UV rays.

Eating healthy food will do good to your eyesight. Remember that vitamins A, C and E are good for eyes. Try to eat food groups that have these vitamins. And you should do eye exercises because exercise protects your eyesight, too. If a person exercises regularly and eats the right kind of food, his eyes will stay in good condition for a long time.

All above are natural ways of eye care that help us keep healthy eyes. Being happy all the time can be helpful to a person's eyesight, too. In a word, eye care is very important, no matter how old a person is.

(　　) 51. _____ is the most important way to protect our eyes.
　　A. Taking medicine　　　　B. Natural eye care
　　C. Seeing the doctor　　　　D. Being happy all the time

(　　) 52. All the following causes can lead to bad eyesight EXCEPT _____.
　　A. age　　　B. computers　　　C. reading　　　D. height

(　　) 53. What should you do if you have to work in front of the computer?
　　A. Eat healthy food.
　　B. Clean the eye by using cold water.
　　C. Wear a pair of sunglasses.
　　D. Have a rest after working for a while.

(　　) 54. What do the underlined words "UV rays" mean in Chinese?
　　A. 紫外线　　　B. 闪电　　　C. 沙尘　　　D. 超声波

(　　) 55. Which is the best title for the passage?
　　A. Ways of Being Happy.　　　B. Ways of Eye Exercises.
　　C. Ways of Eye Care.　　　　 D. Ways of Being Healthy.

第二节　词义搭配：从(B)栏中选出(A)栏单词的正确解释。(共10分，每小题1分)

　　　　(A)　　　　　　　　　(B)

(　　) 56. ignore　　　A. not ill

(　　) 57. illness　　　B. disease; sickness

(　　) 58. reduce　　　C. not private but everyone

( )59. healthy   D. turn a deaf ear to; take no notice of
( )60. handle   E. having less strength
( )61. share   F. use something together
( )62. tired   G. deal with; do with
( )63. effort   H. to gradually grow or become bigger
( )64. public   I. to make less or lower
( )65. develop   J. use strength and energy to do something

第三节　补全对话：根据对话内容，从对话后的选项中选出能填入空白处的最佳选项。(共 10 分，每小题 2 分)

A：Where were you yesterday?

B：___66___

A：Sleep?___67___

B：I was ill, I had a fever. I couldn't get out of bed.

A：___68___ You should go back to bed.

B：I'm going now. I just came here to speak to my professor.

A：___69___

B：He said that I'd be able to take a make-up exam.

A：That's all right then.___70___

B：Ok! Thanks.

> A. Well, take care of yourself.
> B. You still look a little sick.
> C. I was at home asleep.
> D. I thought that you had to take an exam.
> E. What did he tell you?

第三部分　语言技能应用(共分四节，满分 30 分)

第一节　单词拼写：根据下列句子及所给汉语注释，在相应题号后的横线上写出该单词的正确形式。(共 5 分，每小题 1 分)

71. Once he finds _____(压力) in his work, he will give it up.

72. She made an _____(努力) to control her anger.

73. Mary was a good girl with a good _____(脾气).

74. The trip to the seashore brought her out of her _____(抑郁).

75. It is clear that the woman is not a medical _____(技术人员).

第二节　词形变换：用括号内单词的适当形式填空。（共 5 分，每小题 1 分）

76. The green rose is a _____ (develop) from an old kind of rose.

77. They prepare many kinds of Chinese _____ (tradition) food.

78. He likes taking part in all kinds of _____ (active) after class.

79. We suggest that we should tell about his _____ (physics) condition as soon as possible.

80. You can make an _____ (appoint) with the doctor.

第三节　改错：从 A、B、C、D 四个画线处找出一处错误的选项，填入括号内，并在横线上写出正确答案。（共 10 分，每小题 2 分）

81. Why <u>do</u> some <u>animals</u> <u>has</u> two <u>stomaches</u>?
　　　A　　　　B　　　C　　　D

82. They were <u>all</u> very <u>tired</u>, but <u>no one</u> of them stopped to <u>have a rest</u>.
　　　　　A　　　　B　　　C　　　　　　　D

83. <u>There are</u> a lamp, two <u>knives</u> and three books <u>on</u> the desk.
　　A　　B　　　　　　C　　　　　　　　D

84. I <u>think</u> <u>that</u> impossible <u>to finish</u> the work <u>in</u> five days.
　　A　　B　　　　　C　　　　　　D

85. The manager <u>suggested</u> <u>that</u> the work <u>would be</u> finished <u>in</u> two days.
　　　　　A　　　　B　　　　　C　　　　　　D

81.(　)应为_____　82.(　)应为_____　83.(　)应为_____

84.(　)应为_____　85.(　)应为_____

第四节　书面表达。（共 10 分）

作文题目：Health

词数要求：80~100 词

写作要求：1. 说说健康的重要性；

　　　　　2. 谈谈保持健康的方法和建议。

Unit 3

Internship

Warming-up

一、句型汇总

1. A：I want to be... 我想成为……

   B：Then you maybe have your internship in a(n)... 那么你多半在……实习。

2. How is it going with...? ……进展如何?

3. So far, so good. 到目前为止一切都好。

4. It was a challenge at the beginning. 最初对我来说有一点挑战性。

5. It was a little bit...at the beginning. 开始有一点……

6. The staff here were more than happy to offer help. 这里的员工非常乐意帮助我。

7. Do you get along well with...? 你和……相处得好吗?

8. I have to hang up now. 我现在得挂电话了。

9. Practice will turn interns to qualified full-time hires. 实践会让实习生成为合格的全职员工。

10. Trainees will succeed in completing real tasks relating to such majors as... 实习生将成功地完成与……专业学生相关的真实任务。

二、英汉互译

1. three-party-agreement _____
2. _____ (*n.*) 同意→_____ (*v.*) 同意
3. inspection (*n.*) _____
4. train (*v.*) _____ → trainer (*n.*) _____ → trainee (*n.*) _____
5. training plan _____
6. training archive _____
7. _____ 幼儿教师
8. _____ 汽车机械师,汽车修理工
9. _____ (男/女)服务员
10. _____ 幼儿园

Listening and Speaking

一、找出与所给单词画线部分读音相同的选项

( ) 1. org<u>a</u>nize   A. w<u>o</u>rkshop   B. rep<u>o</u>rt   C. w<u>o</u>rd   D. w<u>o</u>rld

( ) 2. r<u>ea</u>l   A. r<u>ea</u>lly   B. t<u>ea</u>cher   C. coll<u>ea</u>gue   D. pl<u>ea</u>se

( ) 3. l<u>ea</u>rn   A. h<u>ea</u>rt   B. cl<u>ea</u>r   C. h<u>ea</u>rd   D. w<u>ea</u>r

( ) 4. forg<u>e</u>t   A. ag<u>e</u>nda   B. probl<u>e</u>m   C. r<u>e</u>ception   D. r<u>e</u>ceive

( ) 5. <u>ch</u>allenge   A. s<u>ch</u>ool   B. stoma<u>ch</u>   C. <u>ch</u>emistry   D. <u>ch</u>eck

二、从(B)栏中找出与(A)栏中相对应的答语

(A)
1. How is it going with your internship?
2. Do you get along well with your colleagues?
3. How do you feel facing real guests?
4. Why didn't he come for our movie activity?
5. Could you please help me?

(B)
A. He was busy. He was preparing for the internship program.
B. So far, so good.
C. Of course! We're friends now.
D. Sure. What happened?
E. It was a challenge at the beginning.

三、用所给句子补全下面对话

Mary: Hi, Mike. __1__

Mike: Hello, Mary! He was busy. He was preparing for the internship program.

Mary: That's great! I just signed my three-party-agreement with our school and my trainer, No. 1 Kindergarten.

Mike: So, __2__

Mary: Yes, but not before I finish the pre-service training program. __3__

Mike: I was thinking of going to a 4S shop at the beginning. But I've changed my mind.

Mary: Why?

Mike: Well, __4__

Mary: Congratulations! By the way, __5__

Mike: Sure. And I've also finished my training plan with my teacher and the trainer.

A. you will be an intern teacher soon?

B. have you checked your insurance?

C. Why didn't Li Ming come for our movie activity?

D. How about you?

E. Hongqi Auto Plant has offered me a better chance to get to know the whole industry.

四、场景模拟

编写一组对话,根据某一实习情境,与同伴进行对话,解决遇到的问题。

提示词汇: the machine stops working suddenly;

cut off the machine's power supply;

report to the workshop director;

contact the maintenance group;

write a brief report after the problem is solved.

Reading and Writing

一、用括号内所给汉语提示或单词的适当形式填空

1. She _____ (major) in Pre-school Education.

2. Trainees will _____ (success) in completing real tasks.

3. He is _____ (dream) to be a teacher.

4. _____ (challenge) are sure to come.

5. Mike is sure to be a _____ (qualify) engineer.

6. Some people might _____ (not agree) with this.

7. We are confident in our _____ (expect) of a full recovery.

8. Good _____ (educate) is the only way to success and independence.

9. Huaxia Company was _____ (found) in 1986.

10. The company is good at _____ (provide) internship programs for vocational school students.

二、完形填空

A big company wanted to find someone to work for them. Lots of young college students came to ask for the 1 . And this time, the company didn't plan to choose the right person as usual. Here came the day when they took the final interview. A big box full of papers was placed on the way to the interview room, and a few 2 were lying around the box.

The 3 student came. He hurried along the way to take the interview. " 4 put the box in the middle of the road?" the student said to himself. But he did not try to move the box away.

The second student came along and did the 5 thing. Then another one came, and another. All of them complained(抱怨) about the box, 6 none of them tried to move it.

Half an hour later, a thin young man with glasses came. He saw the box and papers around it. He stopped to pick up the papers and put 7 in the box. Then he moved the box to the side. 8 his great surprise, he 9 an invitation under the box. It said, "Congratulations! You are the 10 person we are looking for! Would you like to join us?"

Sometimes, you see, helping others is helping yourself.

(　　)1. A. book　　　　B. job　　　　C. money　　　　D. work

(　　)2. A. papers　　　B. books　　　C. magazines　　　D. diaries

(   )3. A. one   B. once   C. first   D. last
(   )4. A. Who   B. When   C. Where   D. What
(   )5. A. different B. common   C. same   D. usual
(   )6. A. but   B. and   C. however   D. so
(   )7. A. it   B. them   C. they   D. its
(   )8. A. To   B. With   C. On   D. Of
(   )9. A. looked   B. invented   C. found   D. heard
(   )10. A. strange   B. right   C. handsome   D. cool

三、阅读理解

阅读下面短文，从每题所给的 A、B、C、D 四个选项中选出最佳答案。

Last year when Jack graduated from school, he came to Shanghai. He didn't like to work on his father's farm and hoped to find a job in a big city. He went from one company to another but no one wanted him. With little money left, he got to the station, sad and tired. All he wanted to do was go back to his small town. It was very late at night and the station was full of people. They were waiting to buy tickets of the last train. He bought the last ticket, and he was very happy.

At that time, a woman with a crying baby walked to him and asked him to sell her the ticket. He gave her the ticket because he thought they needed it more than he did. After the train left, he sat on the bench and didn't know where to go. Suddenly, an old man came and said, "Young man, I have seen what you did to the woman. I am the owner of a big company. I need a good young man like you. Would you like to work for me?"

(   )1. Jack came to the station to _____.
　　A. find a job   B. take the train home
　　C. sell the ticket   D. take the train to Shanghai

(   )2. The woman walked to Jack because _____.
　　A. she was Jack's old friend   B. her child wanted to talk to Jack
　　C. she needed to take the train   D. she had no money to buy a ticket

(   )3. Jack didn't take the train because _____.
　　A. he didn't take a train ticket B. he missed the train
　　C. he wanted to talk to the old man D. he gave his ticket to the woman

(   )4. The old man wanted to _____.
　　A. lend Jack some money   B. give Jack a job
　　C. say "Thank you" to Jack   D. sit on the bench with Jack

( )5. What can we learn from this story?

    A. Many people find job in a train station.

    B. Don't buy the last ticket of the train.

    C. If we try our best to help others, others will help us.

    D. We should not give our ticket to others in a train station.

四、书面表达

利用本单元所学内容试写一篇实习简报。(格式参考教材第 39 页)

_____

_____

_____

_____

_____

_____

Grammar

一、从下面每小题四个选项中选出最佳选项

( )1. I _____ a bath when the telephone rang.

    A. was having   B. have   C. had   D. will have

( )2. When I saw him, he _____ his room.

    A. decorate   B. decorated   C. is decorating   D. was decorating

( )3. She _____ letters. I didn't want to disturb her.

    A. was writing   B. wrote   C. have written   D. is writing

( )4. What _____ she _____ at nine o'clock yesterday?

    A. did; do   B. was; doing   C. has; done   D. does; do

( )5. We _____ TV from six to eight last night.

    A. are watching   B. watch   C. watched   D. were watching

( )6. What _____ he _____ all day last Friday?

    A. did; research   B. does; research

C. was; researching   D. has; researched

( )7. While he was waiting for the bus, he _____ a newspaper.
A. read   B. reads   C. is reading   D. was reading

( )8. He _____ his car while I was cooking.
A. cleaned   B. cleans   C. clean   D. was cleaning

( )9. He _____ in the garden at that moment.
A. was watering   B. watered   C. waters   D. is watering

( )10. Mr. Black _____ in the factory at 6:00 yesterday.
A. work   B. worked   C. is working   D. was working

( )11. At that moment the machine _____ at full speed.
A. ran   B. was running
C. had been running   D. had run

( )12. While the teacher _____ the article, the students _____.
A. was reading; were writing   B. read; wrote
C. was reading; wrote   D. read; was writing

( )13. His room _____ by him when I entered the room.
A. was being cleaned   B. was cleaned
C. was being cleaning   D. has been cleaned

( )14. At this moment yesterday, I _____ housework.
A. am doing   B. was doing   C. did   D. have done

( )15. It _____ when they left the station.
A. was raining   B. rained   C. rains   D. will rain

( )16. When I got to the top of the mountain, the sun _____.
A. shine   B. will shine   C. is shining   D. was shining

( )17. When Mary _____ a dress, she cut her finger.
A. made   B. is making   C. was making   D. makes

( )18. —Do you know our town at all?
—No, this is the first time I _____ here.
A. was   B. have been   C. came   D. am coming

( )19. What _____ you _____ at this time yesterday?
A. were; doing   B. did; do
C. do; do   D. have; done

( )20. While mother _____ Cathy to bed, the door bell _____.
   A. puts; rings   B. put; rang
   C. was putting; rang   D. was putting; was ringing

( )21. I _____ a meal when you _____ me.
   A. cooked; were ringing   B. was cooking; rang
   C. was cooking; were ringing   D. cooked; rang

( )22. He said that he _____ to draw a plane on the blackboard at that time.
   A. tries   B. tried   C. was trying   D. will try

( )23. While she _____ TV, she _____ a sound outside the room.
   A. was watching; was hearing   B. watched; was hearing
   C. watched; heard   D. was watching; heard

( )24. What book _____ you _____ when I _____ you at four yesterday afternoon?
   A. did; read; was seeing   B. did; read; saw
   C. were; reading; saw   D. were; reading; was seeing

( )25. He _____ his father on the farm the whole afternoon last Sunday.
   A. helps   B. would help   C. was helping   D. is helping

( )26. While mother _____ some washing, I _____ a kite for Kate.
   A. did; made   B. was doing; made
   C. was doing; was making   D. did; was making

( )27. This time yesterday Jack _____ his bike. He _____ TV.
   A. repaired, didn't watch   B. was repairing; watched
   C. repaired; watched   D. was repairing; wasn't watching

( )28. They _____ a football game from 9 to 11 last night.
   A. were watching   B. watch
   C. watched   D. are watching

( )29. —Why didn't you go shopping with us yesterday afternoon?
   —I _____ my mother with housework then.
   A. helped   B. was helping   C. had helped   D. have been helping

( )30. —I called you last night, but nobody answered. Where were you then?
   —Oh, I _____ my pet dog in my yard.
   A. walked   B. was walking   C. am walking   D. will walk

二、找出下列句子中错误的选项,并改正过来

1. What did he doing when the teacher came in?
    A   B   C   D

2. He said that he watched TV at nine o'clock the day before.
    A   B   C   D

3. Mother asked me if the Smiths were going to move here long before.
                   A   B   C   D

4. Look! Two hundred students were watching a football match on the playground.
    A   B   C   D

5. The teacher told us that the earth moved around the sun.
        A   B   C   D

6. My parents live in Shanghai with my grandparents now.
              A   B   C   D

7. While I am sleeping, my mother came in.
     A   B   C   D

8. I will go to school by bus if it will rain tomorrow.
   A   B   C   D

9. Weather play an important role in our life.
      A   B C   D

10. He said that he is doing his homework at 7 last night.
              A   B   C   D

1.(　) 应为　　　　　2.(　) 应为　　　　　3.(　) 应为　　　　

4.(　) 应为　　　　　5.(　) 应为　　　　　6.(　) 应为　　　　

7.(　) 应为　　　　　8.(　) 应为　　　　　9.(　) 应为　　　　

10.(　) 应为　　　　

For Better Performance

一、找出与所给单词画线部分读音相同的选项

(　)1. deal   A. colleague   B. dead   C. bread   D. dealt

(　)2. excel   A. excellent   B. express   C. expert   D. example

(　)3. arrange   A. assistant   B. staff   C. active   D. amazing

(　)4. question   A. expectation   B. suggestion C. description D. inspection

(　)5. intern   A. teacher   B. worker   C. farmer   D. prefer

二、英汉互译

1. qualified (a.) _____
2. procedure (n.) _____
3. sign (v.) _____
4. scholarship (n.) _____
5. receive (v.) _____
6. 挑战 (n.) _____
7. 助理 (n.) _____
8. 表达, 呈现 (v.) _____
9. 实习生 (n.) _____
10. 描述 (n.) _____

三、用括号内所给汉语提示或单词的适当形式填空

1. Please remember the new words and _____ (express) in the text.
2. He gave a _____ (describe) of what he had seen.
3. School is the most _____ (challenge) place in the life of youth today.
4. It was a sudden _____ (decide).
5. Our class is an _____ (excellently) one.
6. You must read the _____ (instruct) carefully before you use the machine.
7. He is the president of a large international _____ (organize).
8. They have made an _____ (agree) about the plan.
9. _____ (know) is power.
10. The restaurant is well-known for its good _____ (serve).

四、找出下列句子中错误的选项,并改正过来

1. In recent years, many changes have been taken place in my hometown.
       A   B   C   D

2. The company provided him for a car last summer.
           A   B   C   D

3. Do you mind to show me round your school?
     A   B   C   D

4. If it will be fine tomorrow, we will spend our holiday at the beach.
    A   B   C   D

5. Yesterday I met an old friend of my brother.
          A   B   C   D

1.( ) 应为 _____   2.( ) 应为 _____   3.( ) 应为 _____

4.( ) 应为 _____   5.( ) 应为 _____

单元检测

第一部分　英语知识运用（共分三节，满分40分）

第一节　语音知识：从 A、B、C、D 四个选项中找出其画线部分与所给单词画线部分读音相同的选项。（共 5 分，每小题 1 分）

(　　)1. pr<u>o</u>gram　　A. pr<u>o</u>mote　　B. pr<u>o</u>mise　　C. pr<u>o</u>vince　　D. pr<u>o</u>tect

(　　)2. re<u>c</u>eption　　A. fa<u>c</u>ial　　B. an<u>c</u>ient　　C. <u>c</u>olor　　D. <u>c</u>ertainly

(　　)3. r<u>ea</u>peat　　A. br<u>ea</u>th　　B. ch<u>ea</u>p　　C. br<u>ea</u>kfast　　D. pl<u>ea</u>sure

(　　)4. cou<u>gh</u>　　A. thou<u>gh</u>t　　B. si<u>gh</u>t　　C. enou<u>gh</u>　　D. strai<u>gh</u>t

(　　)5. difficult<u>y</u>　　A. directl<u>y</u>　　B. st<u>y</u>le　　C. fl<u>y</u>　　D. wh<u>y</u>

第二节　词汇与语法知识：从 A、B、C、D 四个选项中选出可以填入空白处的最佳选项。（共 25 分，每小题 1 分）

(　　)6. He is _____ intern from _____ vocational school.
　　A. a; an　　B. an; a　　C. an;／　　D.／;／

(　　)7. The school provides many activities _____ the students.
　　A. to　　B. with　　C. for　　D. of

(　　)8. An advanced diploma course emphasizes high level practical skills in such areas _____ Accounting, Building Design and Engineering.
　　A. as　　B. that　　C. for　　D. to

(　　)9. I didn't hear what you said, because I _____ my teeth at that time.
　　A. brushed　　B. am brushing　　C. was brushing　　D. have brushed

(　　)10. Let's _____ the numbers together and work out a plan.
　　A. go through　　B. go on　　C. go along　　D. go in

(　　)11. _____ in 1986, Huaxia Company is good at providing internship programs for vocational school students.
　　A. Found　　B. Founding　　C. Founded　　D. To found

(　　)12. The Blacks enjoy _____ football games.
　　A. watch　　B. to watch　　C. watching　　D. watched

(　　)13. Li Hua majors _____ Pre-school Education. She can find a suitable position in this program.

Unit 3　Internship

　　　A. in　　　　　B. on　　　　　C. with　　　　D. /

(　)14. His job is to _____ after-sale problems.

　　　A. deal in　　B. deal with　　C. dealt in　　D. dealt with

(　)15. I will keep _____ my English competence.

　　　A. building　　B. building up　　C. build　　D. build up

(　)16. I decided to go to Hongqi Car Factory _____ 4S shop for a better chance to get to know the whole industry.

　　　A. instead　　　　　　　　　B. take the place of

　　　C. take his place　　　　　　D. instead of

(　)17. He _____ the pre-service training session.

　　　A. do well in　B. does well in　C. be good at　D. is good for

(　)18. —Hello. May I speak to Bill, please?

　　　—_____

　　　A. Bill speaking　　　　　　B. I'm Bill

　　　C. You are speaking to Bill　　D. I'm speaking

(　)19. The program _____ a pre-service training program, expressing expectations and role definitions, to get the students prepared for the real deal.

　　　A. start with　B. starts with　C. start　　D. to start

(　)20. The life is full of _____.

　　　A. challenge　B. challenging　C. challenges　D. a challenge

(　)21. Jack _____ as an intern in a small company at this time last winter.

　　　A. was working　B. is working　C. works　　D. worked

(　)22. —What are you doing?

　　　—I'm looking _____ the children. They should be back for lunch now.

　　　A. after　　　B. at　　　　　C. for　　　　D. up

(　)23. The restaurant was _____ in 1980 by a woman cook.

　　　A. set up　　B. set out　　　C. set off　　D. set down

(　)24. As soon as he entered the room, he _____ his cap and sat down.

　　　A. took off　　B. took out　　C. took away　　D. took down

(　)25. Excuse me. _____ you please pass me that cup?

　　　A. Do　　　　B. Should　　　C. Would　　　D. Must

(　)26. All through the morning, she did nothing but _____ on the sofa, watching TV.

　　　　　　A. to sit　　　B. sitting　　　C. sit　　　　D. sat

(　)27. —_____ will you come back?

　　　　—In three days.

　　　　　　A. How often　B. How long　　C. How soon　D. How far

(　)28. _____ happy time we have these days!

　　　　　　A. What　　　B. What a　　　C. How　　　　D. How a

(　)29. Thank you for _____!

　　　　　　A. not smoking　B. smoking not　C. not to smoke　D. to not smoke

(　)30. —Have a nice weekend!

　　　　—_____

　　　　　　A. Thank you.　　　　　　　　B. Why do you say so?

　　　　　　C. Of course, I will be.　　　D. How strange you are!

第三节　完形填空：阅读下面的短文，从所给的 A、B、C、D 四个选项中选出正确的答案。（共 10 分，每小题 1 分）

　　We are in a world __31__ competition. Our parents compete with __32__ in their offices, our brothers and sisters compete with others in their colleges, and we compete with our classmates in school. Most of us give up in the face of competition and will never be __33__. Why can't we do better than others? One important __34__ is that we have no self-confidence.

　　In fact, we are equal when we were birth. You can do __35__ others do. Although your classmates may be better than you __36__ some ways, you may be better than them in other subjects. So __37__ has his or her own advantages. Don't look at things from a single point of view. Try to __38__ your own advantages, and believe that you can do better than others in those ways.

　　Competition is not __39__ terrible. Don't be afraid of it. Don't be afraid those __40__ are more excellent than you. Remember that self-confidence is the first step to success. Believe in yourselves, and you will be successful in any competition.

(　)31. A. full with　　B. full of　　　C. filled of　　　D. fill with

(　)32. A. others　　　B. other　　　 C. another　　　 D. the other

(　)33. A. success　　 B. succeed　　 C. successful　　 D. successfully

(　)34. A. reason　　　B. cause　　　 C. result　　　　D. excuse

(　)35. A. which　　　B. what　　　　C. that　　　　　D. when

(　)36. A. on　　　　　B. at　　　　　C. in　　　　　　D. with

(　)37. A. someone　　 B. anyone　　　C. no one　　　　D. everyone

(　)38. A. find　　　　B. look for　　C. discover　　　D. invent

Unit 3 Internship

(　　)39. A. so　　　　　　B. so a　　　　　C. such a　　　　　D. such

(　　)40. A. which　　　　B. that　　　　　C. who　　　　　　D. whom

第二部分　篇章与词汇理解(共分三节，满分 50 分)

第一节　阅读理解：阅读下列短文，从每题所给的 A、B、C、D 四个选项中，选出最恰当的答案。(共 30 分，每小题 2 分)

A

I often dreamed about Pisa when I was a boy. I read about the famous building called the Leaning Tower of Pisa. But when I read the word Pisa, I Was thinking of pizza. I thought this tower was a place to buy pizza. It must be the best place to buy pizza in the world, I thought.

Many years later I finally saw the Leaning Tower. I knew then that it was Pisa and no pizza. But there was still something special about it for me. The tower got its name because it really did lean to one side. Some people want to try to fix it. They are afraid it may fall over and they don't like it leans over the city.

I do not think it's a good idea to try to fix it. The tower probably will not fall down. It is 600 years old. Why should anything happen to it now? And, if you ask me, I like what it looks like. To me it is a very human kind of leaning. Nothing is perfect. It seems to say.

And who cares? Why do people want things to be perfect? Imperfect things may be more interesting. Let's take the tower in Pisa. Why is it so famous? There are many other older, more beautiful towers in Italy. But Pisa tower is the most famous. People come from all over the world to see it.

(　　)41. This passage is about _____.

　　A. Italian pizza　　　　　　　　B. Italy's problems

　　C. the Leaning Tower of Pisa　　D. why the writer likes pizza

(　　)42. The writer used to think Pisa _____.

　　A. in Spain　　　　　　　　B. not very famous

　　C. not the same as pizza　　D. the same as pizza

(　　)43. The Leaning Tower of Pisa is _____.

　　A. modern　　B. falling down　　C. 600 years old　　D. 60 years old

(　　)44. The writer _____.

　　A. doesn't like what the tower looks like

　　B. likes what the tower looks like

C. thinks it's the most beautiful tower in Italy

D. doesn't like towers

(　　)45. The writer likes the Leaning Tower of Pisa because _____.

A. it's old　　　　　　　　B. it's perfect

C. it sells pizza　　　　　D. it's imperfect

B

A group of old classmates, who have succeeded in their work, got together to visit their teacher. Their conversation soon turned to complaining(抱怨) about the stress(压力) in their work and life. The teacher went to the kitchen and returned with a large pot of coffee and many cups. Some of the cups are expensive and lovely, but some are cheap and not beautiful. The teacher told them to help themselves to the coffee.

When all the students had a cup of coffee in hand the teacher said, "Have you noticed all the nice-looking expensive cups were taken, leaving behind the cheap ones? It's OK for you to want only the best for yourselves, but that is why you have the stress in your work and life even if you're very successful now."

"Now think about this: life is the coffee, and money and position in society are cups. They are just tools to hold life. They do not change the quality(质量) of life. Sometimes, we just care about the cups, and we fail to enjoy the coffee. So don't let the cups drive you, enjoy the coffee instead."

(　　)46. The students who visited the teacher _____.

A. are satisfied with their work　　B. are successful in their studies

C. are strict with each other　　　D. are successful in their work

(　　)47. The teacher took out cups _____.

A. for the students to have coffee　B. to show to the students

C. for the students to have a look　D. to show his favorite coffee

(　　)48. The teacher noticed that the students _____.

A. liked the cheap cups　　　　　B. only took the best cups

C. were drinking coffee　　　　　D. preferred the coffee to cups

(　　)49. Why did the students have the stress in the work and life?

A. Because they wanted coffee.

B. Because they didn't have good cups.

C. Because they didn't pay enough attention to life itself.

D. Because they didn't have money to buy coffee and cups.

( ) 50. From the story, we know the teacher wanted the students to enjoy _____.

A. the cups
B. the coffee
C. life
D. money and position

C

People use their mouths for many things. They eat, talk, shout and sing. They smile and they kiss. In the English language, there are many expressions about the word "mouth". But some of them are not so nice. For example, if you say bad things about a person, the person might protest and say "Do not bad mouth me."

Sometimes, people say something to a friend of family member that they later regret because it hurts that people's feelings. Or they tell the person something they were not supposed to. The speaker might say: "I really put my foot in my mouth this time". If this should happen, the speaker might feel down in the mouth. In other words, he might feel afraid for saying the wrong thing.

Sometimes when one person is speaking, he says the same thing that his friend was going to say. When this happens, the friend might say: "You took the words right out of my mouth!" Sometimes a person has a bad or unpleasant experience with another person. He might say that experience "left a bad taste in my mouth". Or the person has possibly had a very scary experience, like being <u>chased</u> by an angry dog. He might say, "I had my heart in my mouth."

Some people have lots of money because they were born into a very rich family. There is an expression for this, too. You might say such a person "was born with a silver spoon in his mouth". This rich person is the opposite of a person who lives from "hand to mouth". This person is very poor and only has enough money for the most important thing in life, like food.

( ) 51. When a man says "I had my heart in my mouth", usually he means he is _____.

A. excited   B. scared   C. surprised   D. satisfied

( ) 52. Your best friend Tony said what you were going to say, you might say "_____".

A. You were born with a silver spoon in your mouth
B. You really put my foot in my mouth
C. You really left a bad taste in my mouth
D. You took the words right out of my mouth

( ) 53. What does the underlined word "chased" mean in Chinese?

A. 追赶   B. 戏耍   C. 喂食   D. 陪伴

( )54. A person who lives from "hand to mouth" is very _____.
   A. happy   B. healthy   C. poor   D. rich

( )55. According to the passage, _____ are not so nice.
   A. some bad people's mouths
   B. some people using the word "mouth"
   C. some expressions about mouth
   D. some things people use their mouths to do

第二节 词义搭配：从（B）栏中选出（A）栏单词的正确解释。（共 10 分，每小题 1 分）

(A) (B)

( )56. arrangement   A. an amount of money given to sb. by an organization to help pay for their education

( )57. deal   B. a hope that sth. good will happen

( )58. expectation   C. a plan or preparation that you make so that sth. can happen

( )59. guest   D. to buy and sell a particular product

( )60. instruction   E. a person that you have invited to your house

( )61. prize   F. a person whose job is to deal with people arriving at or telephoning a hotel

( )62. scholarship   G. all the workers employed in an organization considered as a group

( )63. receptionist   H. an award that is given to a person who wins a competition, etc.

( )64. staff   I. detailed information on how to do or use sth.

( )65. intern   J. a student or new graduate who is getting practical experience in a job

第三节 补全对话：根据对话内容，从对话后的选项中选出能填入空白处的最佳选项。（共 10 分，每小题 2 分）

A: Hello, Wang Hua! How is it going with your internship?

B: Hi, Mrs Smith. __66__ I've finished the pre-service training organized by the Human Resources Department, and I've learned a lot about working in a real workshop. Now, I'm an assistant operator!

A: Great! __67__

B: Well, I operate real machines and help with the trainer.

A: __68__

B: It was a little bit challenging at the beginning. There's still a lot to learn in the real workplace. I asked many questions, and the staff here were more than happy to offer help.

　　A：___69___

　　B：Of course! We're friends now.

　　A：___70___ See you later, then.

　　B：Bye-bye, Mrs Smith.

> A. Tell me more about it.
> B. Do you get along well with your colleagues?
> C. That's good.
> D. How do you feel operating real machines?
> E. So far, so good

第三部分　语言技能应用(共分四节，满分30分)

第一节　单词拼写：根据下列句子及所给汉语注释，在相应题号后的横线上写出该单词的正确形式。(共5分，每小题1分)

71. Do you get along well with your _____(同事)?

72. The job _____(描述) shows the trainee what to do at the workplace.

73. I will get some _____(职前培训) training next week.

74. This will help me make more _____(进步) in my future career.

75. He was very good at _____(解决) problems.

第二节　词形变换：用括号内单词的适当形式填空。(共5分，每小题1分)

76. You should make _____(prepare) for an internship.

77. It was a challenge at the _____(begin).

78. He was _____(wait) for me at 8 yesterday morning.

79. The tourists felt _____(amaze) at the great changes.

80. He offered many _____(value) ideas to the company.

第三节　改错：从 A、B、C、D 四个画线处找出一处错误的选项，填入括号内，并在横线上写出正确答案。(共10分，每小题2分)

81. A plane is flying highly in the sky.
　　　A　　　B　　C　　D

82. Don't stay at home. You had better to go out for a walk.
　　　　　　A　　　　　　B　　　C　　　D

83. Why do you prefer running than swimming?
　　　A　B　　　C　　　　　D

— 57 —

84. Do you mind to show me round your company?
     A   B   C   D

85. Our city is a modern one. It founded in the early 1980s.
                  A   B   C   D

81.(   )应为_____   82.(   )应为_____   83.(   )应为_____

84.(   )应为_____   85.(   )应为_____

第四节 书面表达。(共 10 分)

题目：An unforgettable internship experience

词数要求：80~100 词

写作要点：1. 描述一次自己的实习经历；

　　　　　2. 说明时间、地点、人物和事件。

Unit 4

Volunteer Work

Warming-up

一、句型汇总

1. I have tried all the means of transportation. 我乘坐过各种交通工具。
2. do some cleaning in a community 在社区里打扫卫生
3. collect plastic bottles 收集塑料瓶
4. visit the elderly in a nursing home 探访养老院的老人
5. be a teacher in rural areas 在农村当老师
6. plant trees on a hill 在山上种树
7. protect animals 保护动物

二、英汉互译

1. 渡轮_____
2. light rail _____
3. beach _____
4. 贡品_____
5. 建筑_____
6. electronic _____
7. 展示_____
8. knowledge _____
9. palace _____
10. public _____

Listening and Speaking

一、找出与所给单词画线部分读音相同的选项

( ) 1. activity   A. amazing   B. application   C. apply   D. architecture

( ) 2. inform   A. organization   B. palace   C. patient   D. responsible

( ) 3. public   A. result   B. graduate   C. curious   D. volunteer

( ) 4. university   A. century   B. rural   C. actual   D. cubism

( ) 5. select   A. media   B. design   C. directly   D. event

二、从(B)栏中找出与(A)栏中相对应的答语

(A)	(B)
1. Would you mind not smoking here?	A. Sorry, I won't.
2. Would you like something to drink?	B. Yes, please.
3. Don't smoke here.	C. Sorry, I will stop right now.
4. Why not go to movies with us?	D. Sounds great.
5. Could you please take out the trash?	E. Sorry, mum. I'm doing my homework.

三、用所给句子补全下面对话

A: Hello, Mary ___1___

B: I went to Kunming on my holiday.

A: ___2___

B: It was warm.

A: ___3___

B: I went there by plane.

A: ___4___

B: I saw folk dances.

A: Did you eat any Kunming's snack?

B: ___5___ They're delicious.

> A. How did you go there?
> B. What did you do there?
> C. What was the weather like?
> D. Where did you go on your holiday?
> E. Yes, I did.

四、书面表达

假如你是 Steve，是志愿者俱乐部的一名成员，你觉得参加志愿者活动是一件有意义的事情，因此你想邀请你的朋友 Brian 一起参加。请根据提示给他写一封信，介绍俱乐部的活动。

要求：80 词左右，可适当发挥。信件的格式和开头已给出，不计入总词数。

Dear Brian,

　　I am a member of the Volunteer Club. I'd like to introduce the activities in the Volunteer Club to you.

_____
_____
_____
_____
_____
_____
_____

Yours,

Steve

Reading and Writing

一、用括号内所给汉语提示或单词的适当形式填空

1. The products of the company sell well both at _____ （国内外）.
2. The students _____ （期待） the opportunity to do some volunteer work.
3. I like history and I will _____ （主修）History in college.
4. A trained dog can _____ （充当）a guide to blind people.

5. If you want to be a cook in that restaurant, you'd better _____（擅长）Western cooking.

6. I am writing to _____（申请）to work as an volunteer for the Great Wall Protection Project.

7. I am helpful and _____（负责的）.

8. I am good at communication and _____（组织）.

9. I hope to learn more about its _____（历史）.

10. And I would like to _____（贡献）to the protection of our cultural heritage.

二、完形填空

阅读下面的短文，从所给的 A、B、C、D 四个选项中选出正确的答案。

Waste can be seen everywhere in the school. Some students ask for __1__ food than they can eat and others often forget __2__ off the lights when they leave the classroom. They say they can afford these things. But I don't agree __3__ them.

Waste can bring a lot of __4__. __5__ China is rich in some resources, we are short of others, for example, fresh water. It's reported that we will have no coal or oil to use in 100 years. So if we go on __6__ our resources, what can we use in the future and where can we move? Think about it. I think we should say "no" to the students __7__ waste things every day. Everybody should stop wasting as soon as possible.

In our everyday life, we can do many things __8__ waste from happening, for example, turn __9__ the water taps when we finish washing, turn off the lights when we leave the classroom, try not to order more food __10__ we need, and so on. Little by little, everything will be changed. Waste can be stopped one day, if we do our best.

(　　) 1. A. many　　　　B. much　　　　C. most　　　　D. more
(　　) 2. A. to turn　　　B. turning　　　C. turned　　　D. turns
(　　) 3. A. to　　　　　B. with　　　　 C. on　　　　　D. for
(　　) 4. A. questions　　B. matters　　　C. problems　　D. events
(　　) 5. A. However　　 B. Although　　 C. But　　　　 D. While
(　　) 6. A. waste　　　　B. to waste　　 C. wasted　　　D. wasting
(　　) 7. A. who　　　　 B. what　　　　C. which　　　D. when
(　　) 8. A. prevent　　　B. have prevented　C. to prevent　D. prevented
(　　) 9. A. off　　　　　B. on　　　　　C. to　　　　　D. back
(　　) 10. A. when　　　 B. what　　　　C. than　　　　D. while

三、阅读理解

One day a rich lawyer was walking through the street of the town where he lived; he was on his way to see his brother who lived some distance from his house. He stopped to watch a man who was beating a donkey with a whip(鞭子). The donkey seemed to take no notice and it was clear that the man was not going to do much better by the method he had used.

After a while the lawyer said to him, "Why are you doing that?"

"To make the donkey go," replied the man.

"Have you had the right to beat the poor animal like that?" asked the lawyer.

"Certainly I have", answered the man. "It is my donkey and I can do what I like with what is mine."

The lawyer thought for a minute and then told the man that he did not think that was really true. But what he said did not seem to persuade the man, so the lawyer took his own stick and started to beat the man about the head and shoulders.

"Stop," cried the man, "What have I done to deserve(应得) this?"

"Oh", replied the lawyer, "this is my stick and I have the right to do what I like what is mine."

( ) 1. The lawyer was on his way to see _____.
  A. his brother B. his parents C. his friend D. his uncle

( ) 2. On his way he saw a man _____ a donkey.
  A. walking by B. whipping C. sitting on D. feeding

( ) 3. He was doing this to make the donkey _____.
  A. stop B. dance C. go D. carry more

( ) 4. The donkey seemed to _____.
  A. enjoy the beating B. be dead
  C. understand his master D. pay no attention

( ) 5. The lawyer didn't think the man _____ beat the donkey like that.
  A. had the right to B. had any reason to
  C. was right to D. needed to

四、书面表达

你校将以六月八日世界海洋日为主题，举办英语征文比赛，请你写一篇短文投稿。内容包括：

1. 海洋的重要性；

2. 保护海洋的倡议。

注意：

词数为 100 词左右。

Grammar

一、从下面每小题四个选项中选出最佳选项

( )1. — _____ interesting movies!
—Yes, everybody likes them.
A. What　　　B. How　　　C. What an　　　D. How an

( )2. _____ new radio it is!
A. How a　　　B. What a　　　C. How　　　D. What

( )3. _____ delicious these beef noodles are!
A. What　　　B. How　　　C. What a　　　D. How a

( )4. _____ interesting book it is! I want to read it again.
A. What an　　　B. How　　　C. What　　　D. How an

( )5. —The summer vacation is coming. Why don't you go to the beach to enjoy the sunshine?
—Sounds great. _____ advice!
A. What good　　　B. How good　　　C. What a good　　　D. How a good

( )6. —Have you watched the boat races this Dragon Boat Festival?
—Yes. _____ wonderful races!
A. What an　　　B. What a　　　C. How　　　D. What

( )7. _____ exciting boat race it was! Many people watched it.
A. What a　　　B. What an　　　C. How　　　D. How an

( )8. _____ fun it is to have a field trip on the Orange Island!

  A. What   B. What a   C. How   D. How a

( )9. _____ food you've cooked!

  A. How a nice   B. What a nice

  C. How nice   D. What nice

( )10. _____ nervous the girl was! She could not fall asleep all night.

  A. What   B. What a   C. How   D. How a

( )11. _____ clever boy he is!

  A. How   B. What   C. What a   D. What an

( )12. —Look at the cloud! It looks like a rabbit.

  —Wow, _____ beautiful!

  A. What   B. What a   C. How   D. How a

( )13. —Wow, my best friend Anna got an A in her test!

  —_____ wonderful news it is!

  A. What   B. What a   C. How   D. How a

( )14. —_____ beautiful place Zhangjiajie is, Lu Ming!

  —Yeah, and thousands of visitors come here to spend their holidays every year.

  A. What a   B. What   C. How   D. How a

( )15. _____ bad weather it is!

  A. How   B. What a   C. What   D. What an

( )16. _____ wonderful book "Gulliver's Travels" is! It became popular as soon as it came out.

  A. How   B. What   C. What a   D. How a

( )17. —_____ fine day! Shall we go for a walk?

  —That sounds great!

  A. What   B. How   C. What a   D. How a

( )18. —Kate has won the first prize in the dancing competition.

  —_____ great surprise this gave her classmates!

  A. What a   B. What   C. How   D. How a

( )19. _____ honest boy he is!

  A. What a   B. How   C. What an   D. How a

( )20. —_____ weather it is! We can't go on a picnic in Fangshan Hill.

  —Don't worry. Let's go to Jiangning Museum instead.

  A. What good   B. How good   C. How bad   D. What bad

(   )21. _____ unforgettable moment it was to the fans of Leonardo Di Caprio around the world!

        A. What   B. How   C. What a   D. What an

(   )22. —_____ unusual music Li Yundi is playing!

    —Yes, all of the students are losing themselves in it.

        A. How   B. What an   C. How a   D. What

(   )23. —So far, Su Bingtian is the only Chinese who finished the 100-meter race in less than 10 seconds.

    —_____ he runs!

        A. How slow   B. How fast

        C. What a slow   D. What a fast

(   )24. _____ pretty the dragon boats are! I am sure the race will be very exciting.

        A. What a   B. How a   C. What   D. How

(   )25. —_____ brave Lin Tao is!

    —Yes, he helped his neighbour, Mrs Sun, out of fire.

        A. How a   B. What   C. What a   D. How

(   )26. —_____ big lanterns! I like them very much!

    —Yes. They sell well in our town.

        A. How   B. What   C. What a   D. What an

(   )27. _____ interesting our school life is!

        A. What an   B. How   C. How an   D. What a

(   )28. _____ strange weather it is.

        A. What a   B. How a   C. What   D. How

(   )29. —The firemen did all their best to put out the fire.

    —_____ excellent firemen!

        A. What   B. What an   C. How an   D. How

(   )30. Look! The model is walking to us. _____ nice dress!

        A. What   B. What a   C. How   D. How a

二、找出下列句子中错误的选项,并改正过来

1. On their way to home, they found a small cat in the tree.
      A   B   C   D

2. The little girl said that she doesn't afraid of fire at all.
                  A   B   C   D

3. Did you do anything for your own safe?
        A   B   C   D

4. How often do you hear a letter from your parents?
      A   B   C   D

5. I have nothing do this evening. Shall we go shopping?
       A   B   C   D

6. Peter's birthday is to December.
      A   B C D

7. What does Tim going to do next sunday?
      A   B   C   D

8. The students is watching a video when the lights went out.
      A   B   C   D

9. I made such many mistakes that I didn't pass the exam.
     A   B   C   D

10. There have a class meeting next Monday afternoon.
         A B   C   D

1. (　) 应为_____　　2. (　) 应为_____　　3. (　) 应为_____
4. (　) 应为_____　　5. (　) 应为_____　　6. (　) 应为_____
7. (　) 应为_____　　8. (　) 应为_____　　9. (　) 应为_____
10. (　) 应为_____

For Better Performance

一、找出与所给单词画线部分读音相同的选项

(　) 1. track　　A. data　　B. activity　　C. pace　　D. organize

(　) 2. cycle　　A. family　　B. apply　　C. exactly　　D. fly

(　) 3. series　　A. amazing　　B. request　　C. gas　　D. discussion

(　) 4. steam　　A. great　　B. bread　　C. weather　　D. beach

(　) 5. shock　　A. recover　　B. found　　C. knowledge　　D. go

二、英汉互译

1. public _____　　2. 知识_____

3. 活动_____　　4. result_____

5. major_____　　6. palace_____

7. be skilled in _____　　8. 充当_____

9. 组织_____　　10. 基础教育_____

三、用所给单词的适当形式填空

1. I'd like to be a volunteer at a rural _____(element) school.
2. We need people who are _____(help).
3. We are looking forward to your _____(参与).
4. You will be informed when and where to have a _____(write) test and an interview.
5. December 5th is the _____(国际性) Volunteer Day.
6. It makes you feel like a better and _____(use) person to society.
7. I would like to contribute to the protection of our _____(文化) heritage.
8. Some _____(volunteer) help out with the daily care of the animal.
9. They enjoyed _____(oneself).
10. He went down his _____(knee) to sweep the floor.

四、找出下列句子中错误的选项，并改正过来

1. This is the factory where we visited last week.
    A   B   C   D
2. This is the watch for which Tom is looking.
      A   B   C   D
3. The person to who you spoke is a student of Grade Two.
  A   B   C   D
4. The house in that we live is very small.
  A   B   C D
5. The sun gives off light and warmth, that makes it possible for plants to grow.
       A   B   C   D

1.(　　)应为_____　　2.(　　)应为_____　　3.(　　)应为_____
4.(　　)应为_____　　5.(　　)应为_____

单元检测

第一部分　英语知识运用(共分三节，满分40分)

第一节　语音知识：从 A、B、C、D 四个选项中找出其画线部分与所给单词画线部分读音相同的选项。(共5分，每小题1分)

(　　)1. application　　A. activity　　B. amazing　　C. apply　　D. architecture
(　　)2. tea　　A. breath　　B. bread　　C. sweater　　D. beach
(　　)3. department　　A. best　　B. section　　C. report　　D. definition

(   )4. collect　　　A. tomato　　B. go　　　　C. note　　D. both

(   )5. gain　　　　A. against　　B. pain　　　C. captain　D. curtain

第二节　词汇与语法知识：从 A、B、C、D 四个选项中选出可以填入空白处的最佳选项。(共 25 分，每小题 1 分)

(   )6. —We are moving to Maimi next week, Marilyn!
　　　　—_____!
　　　　A. Take your time　B. All the best　　C. Well done　　D. That's OK

(   )7. My brother is so interested in languages that he is now learning _____ third language besides English and French.
　　　　A. 不填　　　B. the　　　　C. a　　　　D. that

(   )8. —Hi, sir, may I _____ seats with you? I want to sit next to my mother.
　　　　—With pleasure.
　　　　A. give　　　B. take　　　C. exchange　　D. have

(   )9. With winter _____, the weather gets colder and colder.
　　　　A. appearing　　B. approaching　　C. leaving　　D. passing

(   )10. He is poor in money, but rich in _____.
　　　　A. knowledge　　B. communications　　C. attention　　D. business

(   )11. The music played by Lang Lang _____ very pleasing to the ear.
　　　　A. sounds　　B. hears　　C. listens　　D. listens to

(   )12. —How's Jack doing in Britain?
　　　　—I wrote an email to him last week, but _____ I have had no reply from him.
　　　　A. from now on　B. so far　　C. just now　　D. later on

(   )13. Only one child of the thirty passengers in the plane _____ after the air crash.
　　　　A. survived　　B. starved　　C. shouted　　D. shook

(   )14. —Shall I get you something to drink?
　　　　—Thanks, but don't _____. I have to leave now.
　　　　A. make　　　B. annoy　　C. disturb　　D. bother

(   )15. My family used to live in _____ city of Shanghai but now have moved to _____ countryside.
　　　　A. a; a　　　B. the; the　　C. a; the　　D. the; 不填

(   )16. Nobody wants to _____ especially in public.
　　　　A. make fun of　　　　　B. be made fun of
　　　　C. making fun of　　　　D. made fun of

( )17. —How long are you staying?

—I don't know. _____

A. That's OK.　　B. It depends.　　C. I am going.　　D. It's doesn't matter.

( )18. Tom is _____ repairing computers.

A. skilled in　　B. skill in　　C. skilled at　　D. skill of

( )19. The store has an excellent _____ for fair dealing and its booming sales figures are often reported in local newspapers.

A. regulation　　B. reputation　　C. presentation　　D. expectation

( )20. Both his parents look sad. Maybe they _____ what's happened to him.

A. knew　　B. have known　　C. must know　　D. will know

( )21. —*Harry Potter* is very interesting and it is one of the most popular books in the world.

—_____ And I don't know why so many people are interested in it.

A. That sounds great.　　B. I can believe that.

C. I just don't like it.　　D. It is not true.

( )22. —Has Lucy ever been to Beijing?

—No, _____.

A. she has　　B. she isn't　　C. she hasn't　　D. she didn't

( )23. —_____ has he stayed in that mountain?

—For a week.

A. How often　　B. How soon　　C. How long　　D. How many

( )24. The movie is so interesting that _____ people have seen it in the past few days.

A. two million　　B. two millions　　C. two million of　　D. two millions of

( )25. Allan was born in America, but he _____ in England.

A. went back　　B. grew up　　C. picked up　　D. turned down

( )26. I have read *Robinson Crusoe* _____, but I haven't read *Tom Sawyer* _____.

A. already; already　　B. yet; yet

C. yet; already　　D. already; yet

( )27. _____! The train is coming!

A. Wake up　　B. Get up　　C. Turn up　　D. Hurry up

( )28. The storybook _____ Lucy. Don't take it away without telling her.

A. is　　B. belongs to　　C. was　　D. belongs with

( )29. —I don't know your friend. Can you _____ her to me?

　　　　—Sure, I can.

　　　　A. introduce　　　B. lead　　　C. let　　　D. meet

( )30. The temperature will fall sharply the day after tomorrow, when a snow storm _____ to strike our area.

　　　　A. expects　　　B. is expected　　　C. has expected　　　D. will be expected

第三节　完形填空：阅读下面的短文，从所给的 A、B、C、D 四个选项中选出正确的答案。（共 10 分，每小题 1 分）

When my son Gene was about 12 years old I started helping him learn to work. I bought twenty chickens and asked him to __31__ them. I told him that they would be his own chickens and we would __32__ the eggs from him. However he would have to buy chicken __33__ with the money he made from the eggs. Whatever money was __34__ would be his to keep. Gene was thrilled thinking he would make his first __35__.

After several weeks' successful work I began to __36__ that egg production was going down I __37__ nothing about it. Then one night Gene told me he didn't have __38__ money to buy the feed. He said the chickens had never __39__ a meal and he could not figure out why some of them had stopped __40__ eggs.

( )31. A. take care of　　B. observe　　C. train　　D. pay attention to

( )32. A. enjoy　　B. borrow　　C. buy　　D. keep

( )33. A. nest　　B. soup　　C. meat　　D. feed

( )34. A. given back　　B. picked up　　C. left over　　D. brought in

( )35. A. deal　　B. contribution　　C. fortune　　D. choice

( )36. A. hear　　B. notice　　C. predict　　D. imagine

( )37. A. said　　B. found　　C. thought　　D. recalled

( )38. A. prize　　B. lucky　　C. pocket　　D. enough

( )39. A. missed　　B. wasted　　C. saved　　D. finished

( )40. A. hatching　　B. laying　　C. bringing　　D. hiding

第二部分　篇章与词汇理解（共分三节，满分 50 分）

第一节　阅读理解：阅读下列短文，从每题所给的 A、B、C、D 四个选项中，选出最恰当的答案。（共 30 分，每小题 2 分）

A

Computers are very important in our life. People can search for information, send emails and do many other things on the computer. Many people shop on the Internet, because they have no time to go shopping. But there are still many people shopping in the shops. We have got some data in a survey. Let's have a look!

45% of the people like shopping on the Internet and 55% of the people like shopping in the shops.

64% of the people learn about things on the Internet before buying them in the shops.

71% of the women buy things on the Internet, but only 52% of the men do this.

Why do many people shop in the shops? Some people don't want to wait for their things to arrive. And some want to see the real things before buying them. What do you think of it?

(　　)41. Many people like shopping on the Internet because they're _____.
　　A. funny　　B. tired　　C. busy　　D. different

(　　)42. If there are 100 people _____, of them like shopping on the Internet according to the survey.
　　A. 45　　B. 55　　C. 52　　D. 71

(　　)43. _____ can help people learn about things before buying them.
　　A. Watching TV　　B. Going on the Internet
　　C. Reading a book　　D. Writing email

(　　)44. _____ of the women shop in the shops.
　　A. 64%　　B. 71%　　C. 48%　　D. 29%

(　　)45. We can see the passage in a _____.
　　A. dictionary　　B. Chinese book　　C. newspaper　　D. science book

B

Mrs. Green lives in a small village. Her husband is dead. But she has a son. He is twenty-one and his name is Jack. He gets work in a town and lives there. Its name is Greensea. It is quite a long way from his mother's village, and she is not happy about this, but Jack says, "There isn't any good work for me in the village, mother, and I can get a lot of money in Greensea and give you some every week."

One day Mrs. Green is very angry. She gets on a train and goes to her son's house in Greensea. Then she says to him, "Jack, why do you never give me a ring?"

Jack laughs and says, "But, mother, you don't have a telephone."

"No," she says, "I don't have one, but you have one."

(　　)46. Where does Mrs. Green live?
　　A. In a big city.　　B. In a small village.
　　C. In a town with his son.　　D. We don't know.

(   )47. How old is Mrs. Green's son?

　　　　A. Twelve.　　B. Twenty.　　　C. Twenty-one.　　D. Thirty-one.

(   )48. Which of these is not wrong?

　　　　A. Greensea is the name of a factory.

　　　　B. Jack works in a town and his mother is happy about this.

　　　　C. In the village there is no good work for Jack.

　　　　D. He can get less money in the town than in the village.

(   )49. How does the woman go to Greensea one day?

　　　　A. On a bike.　　B. On foot.　　C. By train.　　D. By bus.

(   )50. Why does Jack never telephone his mother?

　　　　A. Because he is too busy.

　　　　B. Because he lives far from his mother's village.

　　　　C. Because he doesn't have a telephone.

　　　　D. Because his mother has no telephone.

C

Today I went to Sam's school in the UK. It was really different from my school in China.

Girls wore grey skirts and white shirts, boys wore grey trousers, and everyone wore the school tie.

Some of Sam's lessons were a bit strange for me. We were reading Shakespeare in the English lesson, and there were quite some old words like "thou" and "thee" to mean "you". In history we studied 20th-century China. It was strange hearing a foreign side of history and hearing English people trying to say all our Chinese names!

Classes were also a lot more relaxing than in China. Teachers were called "sir" or "miss". Everyone shouted answers and raised their hands in classes. It was more like a debate than a class. A bell rang at the end of each lesson and everyone jumped up to go to the next class.

At break we bought potato chips and cookies in the dining room. Lunch was later than in China at 1 o'clock. We had big plates of pie with carrots. For dessert there was hot sweet rice called rice pudding.

It was good that I'd had an excellent lunch, because at Sam's school Monday afternoons are taken up with sports.

(   )51. The underlined word "debate" in Paragraph 4 means _____.

　　　　A. fight　　　B. exam　　　C. discussion　　　D. suggestion

(   )52. What do students have for lunch at Sam's school?

　　　　A. Pie and hot sweet rice.　　　　B. Potato chips.

C. Cookies.   D. Carrots.

( )53. What class do Sam have on Monday afternoon?
  A. Maths.   B. History.   C. PE.   D. Music.

( )54. Which of the following is NOT true according to the passage?
  A. Students wear uniforms in Sam's school.
  B. Lessons are different between schools in China and the UK.
  C. Chinese students usually have lunch before 1 o'clock in the school.
  D. Sports take up few time in Sam's school.

( )55. What's the best title for the passage?
  A. Relaxed classes in the UK.
  B. Clothes, food and sports in a UK school.
  C. Strange lessons in Sam's school.
  D. A day in Sam's school.

第二节 词义搭配：从(B)栏中选出(A)栏单词的正确解释。(共10分，每小题2分)

　　　　(A)　　　　　　　　　　(B)

( )56. powerful   A. an organization for business
( )57. perfect   B. keep someone or something safe
( )58. respect   C. have a lot of power to control people or events
( )59. silent   D. to have ability to be good at sth.
( )60. company   E. quiet
( )61. university   F. fit
( )62. talent   G. important
( )63. suitable   H. show admiration to sb.
( )64. major   I. persons or things without fault
( )65. protect   J. a collection of colleges

第三节 补全对话：根据对话内容，从对话后的选项中选出能填入空白处的最佳选项。
(共10分，每小题2分)

M: I'd like a haircut, please.
W: Would you care for a shave and a shampoo as well?
M: No, thanks. A haircut will be just fine.
W: All right. 66
M: Don't cut it too short on the sides and the back. Just a little.
W: 67
M: You can thin the top out a little, but just a little.

W: No problem.

M: My hair is kind of oily, and dandruff（头皮屑）bothers me very much. __68__

W: __69__ It's supposed to be good for the dandruff.

M: No. I've heard of it, but I haven't had a try.

W: And you can try Vidal Sassoon. It's used after you wash your hair. __70__

M: That's a good idea. Thank you.

W: It's done. That will be five dollars and thirty cents.

> A. Have you tried Head and Shoulders?
> B. It will keep your hair oil free.
> C. What hairstyle do you like?
> D. Can you recommend me something effective?
> E. How about the top?

第三部分 语言技能应用（共分四节，满分30分）

第一节 单词拼写：根据下列句子及所给汉语注释，在相应题号后的横线上写出该单词的正确形式。（共5分，每小题1分）

71. I think he did it on _____（目的）.

72. Many people were killed or _____（受伤的）during the earthquake.

73. In class, you should be _____（活跃的）in answering the questions your teacher asks.

74. She comes from London; her _____（天生的）language is English.

75. The weather _____（预报）is not always accurate either.

第二节 词形变换：用括号内单词的适当形式填空。（共5分，每小题1分）

76. Mr. White gave lucy a nice gift and she _____（thank）him very much.

77. The suspect was seen _____（hit）that young woman in the street at that time.

78. It is the second time lucy has _____（ride）to school on her own.

79. To do this would be to _____（cut）the foot to fit the shoe.

80. The paintings he devoted all his life to were _____（show）successful last week.

第三节 改错：从A、B、C、D四个画线处找出一处错误的选项，填入括号内，并在横线上写出正确答案。（共10分，每小题2分）

81. She <u>hurt</u> <u>her</u> when she <u>played</u> <u>with</u> a knife.
    A B   C   D

82. The boy <u>was</u> nine <u>years</u> old <u>and</u> yesterday was his <u>nine</u> birthday.
           A   B   C   D

83. They were made worked day and night those days.
                A   B   C   D

84. I won't watch the TV play if my father let me do my homework.
               A   B   C D

85. Because he hurt his foot, so he could not play with us.
             A   B   C   D

81.(　　)应为_____　　82.(　　)应为_____　　83.(　　)应为_____

84.(　　)应为_____　　85.(　　)应为_____

第四节　书面表达。(共10分)

假如你是社区的社工，就广场舞现象写一篇倡议书，简述广场舞的优点、缺点，倡议大家文明开展广场舞活动。

作文题目自拟。

词数要求：80~100词。

Unit 5

Ancient Civilization

Warming-up

一、句型汇总

1. So how long have you prepared for this exhibition? 你为这次展览准备了多久呢?

2. Which artist or works impress you most in the exhibition? 展览中哪位艺术家或者哪幅作品你印象最深刻呢?

3. I think I am most attracted to the works of the Spanish painter Pablo Picasso, the originator of Cubism. 我认为我最喜欢西班牙画家、立体主义运动创始人巴勃罗·毕加索的作品。

4. He is thought to be one of the greatest artists and sculptors of the 20th century. 他被认为是20世纪最伟大的画家和雕塑家之一。

5. I think even today we are influenced by his ideas. 时至今日我们依然受他的思想所影响。

6. Did you know that the Silk Road was neither an actual road nor a single route? 你知道吗,丝绸之路既不是一条真正意义上的道路,也不是一条单一的路线。

7. The ancient Silk Road also has a long history. 古丝绸之路也有着悠久的历史。

8. These inventions helped boost the development of Western societies. 这些发明促进了西方社会的发展。

9. The Silk Road was a path of cultural exchanges between the East and the West. 丝绸之路是东西方文化交流的通道。

二、英汉互译

1. actual（adj.）_____ →实际上，事实上（adv.）_____
2. artist（n.）_____
3. 吸引（v.）_____ →有魅力的（adj.）_____
4. character（n.）_____
5. 文明（n.）_____
6. curious（adj.）_____ →好奇心（n.）_____
7. 交流；交换（n.）_____
8. exhibition（n.）_____
9. 使留下印象（v.）_____ →印象（n.）_____
10. treasure（n.）_____

Listening and Speaking

一、找出与所给单词画线部分读音相同的选项

( ) 1. <u>a</u>ctual　　A. <u>a</u>dult　　B. <u>a</u>bove　　C. <u>a</u>dvise　　D. <u>a</u>nother

( ) 2. b<u>oo</u>st　　A. l<u>oo</u>k　　B. b<u>oo</u>k　　C. c<u>oo</u>k　　D. f<u>oo</u>d

( ) 3. <u>ex</u>change　　A. <u>ex</u>am　　B. <u>ex</u>ample　　C. <u>ex</u>pression　　D. <u>ex</u>it

( ) 4. l<u>i</u>vely　　A. g<u>i</u>ft　　B. sk<u>i</u>ll　　C. un<u>i</u>versity　　D. m<u>i</u>nd

( ) 5. p<u>ea</u>k　　A. r<u>ea</u>dy　　B. sp<u>ea</u>k　　C. br<u>ea</u>kfast　　D. tr<u>ea</u>sure

二、从（B）栏中找出与（A）栏中相对应的答语

(A)	(B)
1. How long have you been a teacher?	A. It's five to ten.
2. Shall we watch a movie tonight?	B. Well, this is a well-known ancient Chinese painting.
3. When will you arrive in Beijing?	C. For six years.
4. When did you begin to paint?	D. I'd love to.
5. Could you tell me something about Qing Ming Shang He Tu?	E. At the age of 6.

三、用所给句子补全下面对话

Receptionist: Good afternoon. 1

Jason: Could you tell me where the Silk Road exhibition is?

Receptionist: It's in Gallery N1. 2

Jason: Oh, thanks. Can I take photos in the exhibition?

Receptionist: 3

Jason: I see. Are there any guided tours for the exhibition?

Receptionist: 4 You can get the information from the information board at the entrance of the gallery.

Jason: Great. Thank you so much.

Receptionist: You're welcome. 5

> A. Enjoy your visit!
> B. You can take photos, but you can't use the flash.
> C. How can I help you?
> D. There's a guided tour every hour.
> E. Here's a map of the museum to help you find it.

四、场景模拟

编写一组对话,向你的国外朋友介绍长城。

提示词汇: the Great Wall; be located in…; …has a long history; during the waring states period; protect these states.

_____
_____
_____
_____
_____
_____

Reading and Writing

一、用括号内所给汉语提示或单词的适当形式填空

1. What impresses you most in the _____(展览).
2. What were his _____(真实的)words.
3. Germany is a _____(west)country.
4. There is a _____(海事的)museum in the center of the city.
5. He was sent to Africa as an _____(使者).
6. Mona Lisa(蒙娜丽莎)is one of the most famous _____(paint)in the world.
7. He has a good _____(记忆).
8. She is very _____(live)and full of fun.
9. She is a very _____(attract)woman.
10. Chinese _____(文明)is one of the oldest in the world.

二、完形填空

Do you know "One Belt, One Road"? We also call it the Modern Silk Road. And Zhang Qian was an early traveller of the Ancient Silk Road. He was probably the first __1__ to bring back good information about the central Asian lands to China.

In 139 BC, Han Wudi sent Zhang Qian to the Yue-zhi people to ask for their __2__ against the Xiongnu people who often infringed(侵犯)them. __3__, on the way to the Western Regions, he was caught by the Xiongnu people. Zhang had to stay with them __4__ about 10 years before he got away. When Zhang finally __5__ the Yue-zhi people in the North India, he was __6__ to find that they didn't want to fight against the Xiongnu people.

On __7__ return journey, Zhang Qian and his men were __8__ again. It was not until 125 BC that they returned to China. __9__ Zhang didn't finish his job, he learned a lot about the places, people, customs and cultures of the 36 kingdoms(王国)in the Western Regions.

Later Han Wudi sent Zhang to West again. Zhang's journey to the West helped __10__ international trade, especially in silk, between China and the West, That's the Ancient Silk Road.

( )1. A. men   B. man's   C. man   D. men's
( )2. A. question   B. help   C. knowledge   D. answer
( )3. A. Happily   B. Excitedly   C. Luckily   D. Unfortunately

Unit 5　Ancient Civilization

(　　)4. A. for　　　　　B. since　　　　　C. at　　　　　D. in
(　　)5. A. arrived　　　B. reached　　　　C. got　　　　 D. liked
(　　)6. A. comfortable　B. disappointed　　C. excited　　 D. enjoyable
(　　)7. A. him　　　　 B. he　　　　　　 C. his　　　　 D. himself
(　　)8. A. caught　　　B. made　　　　　C. served　　　D. heard
(　　)9. A. But　　　　 B. As　　　　　　C. Because　　　D. Although
(　　)10. A. use　　　　B. get　　　　　　C. develop　　　D. see

三、阅读理解

阅读下面短文，从每题所给的 A、B、C、D 四个选项中选出最佳答案。

Have you ever walked along the Silk Road? Do you know the famous Silk Road? The Silk Road was an ancient network of trade routes（贸易路线）connecting the East and the West.

People used to do business with others from different countries along these routes. Scientists and archaeologists（考古学家）believe people began to travel along the Silk Road centuries ago. By the time the Chinese silk trade became important in the world, the Silk Road had covered almost 6,500 kilometers. It started from China and finally got to Rome.

Merchants traveling along the Silk Road carried silk, of course. They also carried and traded in tea, cloth, gold, jewels and other things. During its busiest time, the Silk Road attracted（吸引）people from many different countries, such as China, Iraq, Turkey and Greece. All those people traveled along the Silk Road to share goods, stories, ideas, languages and cultures.

In modern times, the old Silk Road is still useful, but now people use trains instead of camels and horses to travel. They have realized the Silk Road is becoming more and more important among countries. So they, especially Chinese people, are trying to make better use of it. There is even a Silk Route Museum in Jiuquan, Gansu Province. It has over 35,000 objects about the Silk Road. In this way, China protects the history of many countries.

(　　)1. The old Silk Road started from China and got to _____.
　　A. Iraq　　　　B. Turkey　　　　C. Greece　　　　D. Rome

(　　)2. The underlined word "Merchants" means "_____" in Chinese.
　　A. 流浪汉　　　B. 犯人　　　　　C. 商人　　　　　D. 铁匠

(　　)3. All people could share _____ through the Silk Road.
　　A. families　　B. cultures　　　　C. people　　　　D. countries

(　　)4. What can we infer according to the passage?
　　A. We can get to any part of the world along the Silk Road.
　　B. The Silk Road is playing an important role in the world.

C. Only China would like to make better use of the Silk Road.

D. The Silk Route Museum in Jiuquan simply protects China's history.

(   )5. What's the best title for this passage?

A. The Silk Road.　　　　　　　B. The Silk Route Museum.

C. The East and the West.　　　D. Trades Among Countries.

四、书面表达

以"The Silk Road"为题,写一篇文章,词数为80~100词。

_____
_____
_____
_____
_____
_____
_____

Grammar

一、从下面每小题四个选项中选出最佳选项

(   )1. —I don't know _____ to remember the new English words.

—Don't worry! Try thinking about their pronunciations.

A. what　　　B. how　　　C. where　　　D. why

(   )2. —I wonder _____ Tom gets on so well with his friends.

—Because he is always ready to help others.

A. whether　　　B. when　　　C. how　　　D. why

(   )3. —I think it's going to be a big problem.

—I wonder _____ we can do about it.

A. when　　　B. where　　　C. if　　　D. what

(   )4. —Could you please tell me _____ we will spend our holiday?

—Maybe in the mountains.

A. where　　　B. what　　　C. how　　　D. when

Unit 5 Ancient Civilization

(   ) 5. —Hi, Jim. I hear that you've just come back from Sanya. I'm calling to ask _____.
—Great!
A. how did you visit the city
B. how many days you've spent there
C. which hotel you stayed in Sanya
D. how you found the seafood there

(   ) 6. —I'm going to give a talk on the Dragon Boat Festival to the exchange students.
—Great! But don't forget to tell them _____.
A. what should they eat at the festival
B. why people enjoy the full moon
C. what kind of race is often held
D. How do people celebrate it

(   ) 7. —Mr. Wang, could you tell me how long _____ the magazines?
—At most ten days.
A. I can borrow   B. can I borrow
C. I can keep   D. can I keep

(   ) 8. —I don't know Kate's address. Do you know _____?
—Sorry, I don't know, either.
A. why she lives there   B. why does she live there
C. where she lives   D. where does she live

(   ) 9. —Dad, can you tell me _____? I miss her very much.
—Next month, dear.
A. when my mum will come back   B. when will my mum come back
C. how my mum goes to work   D. where will my mum go

(   ) 10. —Do you know _____ this afternoon?
—I'm not sure, but I'll tell you as soon as she _____.
A. how will Betty arrive; starts
B. how Betty will arrive; will start
C. what time will Betty arrive; will start
D. what time Betty will arrive; starts

(   ) 11. —Jack, could you tell me _____ for travelling this summer?
—We plan to go and see the beautiful sea in Hainan.
A. where your family will go   B. where will your family go

C. how your family will go   D. how will your family go

( ) 12. —What did Max just say to you?

—He asked me _____.

A. if I would like to go skating

B. when did I buy this CD

C. where I will spend the weekend

D. that I had a good time

( ) 13. —David, could you tell me _____?

—Every four years.

A. when the 2026 World Cup will finish

B. how often the World Cup takes place

C. how many teams take part in the World Cup

D. who may score the most goals in the World Cup

( ) 14. —Kitty, do you know _____?

—Sure, about forty minutes.

A. when did their class meeting begin

B. where their class meeting was held

C. how often their class meeting is held

D. how long their class meeting will last

( ) 15. —Could you please tell me _____?

—By taking an online tour.

A. in which way can I improve my writing skills

B. how I can travel around the world in eight hours

C. what places of interest we can visit at a time

D. how should I get some more useful information

( ) 16. —Richard is studying in Germany. I wonder _____.

—On the phone.

A. how his parents keep in touch with him

B. why his parents keep in touch with him

C. how do his parents keep in touch with him

D. why do his parents keep in touch with him

( ) 17. —I don't understand _____.

—I'm sorry. But I was doing my homework at that time.

A. why you didn't watch the football match

B. why didn't you watch the football match

C. why you don't watch the football match

D. why don't you watch the football match

(　　)18. —Excuse me, could you tell me _____?

—In five minutes.

A. how soon will the film begin　　B. how soon the film will begin

C. how long the film has been on　　D. how long has the film been on

(　　)19. —Daniel, could you tell me _____?

—Certainly, in three North American countries: the united states, Mexico, and Canada.

A. when the 2026 Olympics will be held

B. when will the 2026 Olympics be held

C. where the 2026 Olympics will be held

D. where will the 2026 Olympics be held

(　　)20. —Would you please tell me _____?

—Bus No. 22 will take you there.

A. who will we go with to Meilanfang Theater

B. what can we see in Qinghu Wetland Park

C. when we will leave for the Water Forest

D. how we can get to the Old Street

(　　)21. I know he's been curious about everything, but that's _____. Be patient!

A. what do kids like　　B. what kids like

C. what are kids like　　D. what kids are like

(　　)22. —Could you tell me _____?

—At a robot shop.

A. where did Mr. Jiang buy the robot

B. where Mr. Jiang bought the robot

C. why Mr. Jiang bought the robot

D. why did Mr. Jiang buy the robot

(　　)23. —Can you tell me _____? I want to pay a visit to him.

—He just lives opposite our school.

A. where does Jim live　　B. where did Jim live

C. where Jim lives　　D. where Jim lived

(   )24. —Could you please tell me _____?
　　　—OK. I will go to Beijing next week.
　　　A. where will you go　　　　　B. how you will go to Beijing
　　　C. when you will go to Beijing　D. why will you go to Beijing

(   )25. —Could you please tell me where _____? The boss is waiting for him.
　　　A. has Tom gone　　　　　B. Tom has gone
　　　C. has Tom been　　　　　D. Tom has been

(   )26. —What time shall we leave for the airport?
　　　—It's foggy today. I'm not sure _____ be closed soon. Let's go now.
　　　A. whether the highway will　　B. whether will the highway
　　　C. when the highway will　　　D. when will the highway

(   )27. —Could you tell me _____?
　　　—Sure. Walk straight along this street and you'll find it.
　　　A. how can I get to the post office
　　　B. where is the post office
　　　C. which is the way to the post office
　　　D. how far the post office is

(   )28. —Do you know _____ the man in a hat is?
　　　—I'm not sure. Maybe an engineer.
　　　A. who　　　B. what　　　C. which　　　D. whose

(   )29. —Could you tell me _____ get to the mall?
　　　—Sorry. I'm new here. You can ask the man over there.
　　　A. how I can　　B. how to　　C. how　　D. A and B

(   )30. —Granny, the school trip was very exciting but a little tiring.
　　　—Oh, could you tell me _____?
　　　A. how did you go to the park
　　　B. what you did in the trip
　　　C. that you saw something beautiful
　　　D. if your friends had played with you

二、找出下列句子中错误的选项，并改正过来

1. He is wondering when can he finish this difficult job.
　　　　　　A　　　B　　C　　　　　　D

2. We don't know that he did yesterday.
　　A　　　　B　　C　　D

3. The man <u>asked</u> <u>if</u> there <u>is</u> a park <u>near</u> here.
                      A   B   C   D

4. I don't <u>understand</u> <u>why</u> <u>did John ask</u> such a <u>silly</u> question in class yesterday.
              A   B   C   D

5. <u>Could</u> you tell <u>me</u> <u>if</u> he <u>goes</u> to the post office or not?
    A   B C   D

6. I don't <u>remember</u> <u>where</u> <u>did I</u> <u>put</u> the book yesterday.
          A   B   C   D

7. Our teacher told <u>us</u> that sound <u>travelled</u> <u>much</u> more <u>slowly</u> than light.
                A   B   C   D

8. He <u>asked</u> the students <u>what</u> <u>they</u> <u>will</u> play at the talent show.
     A   B   C   D

9. The headmaster <u>hopes</u> everything <u>went</u> <u>well</u>.
                 A   B   C

10. <u>Could</u> you tell <u>me</u> <u>what</u> <u>to</u> get to the station?
     A   B   C   D

1.(　　)应为_____ 2.(　　)应为_____ 3.(　　)应为_____
4.(　　)应为_____ 5.(　　)应为_____ 6.(　　)应为_____
7.(　　)应为_____ 8.(　　)应为_____ 9.(　　)应为_____
10.(　　)应为_____

For Better Performance

一、找出与所给单词画线部分读音相同的选项

(　　) 1. attr<u>a</u>ctive   A. <u>a</u>rtist   B. <u>a</u>ctive   C. <u>a</u>bout   D. d<u>a</u>te

(　　) 2. te<u>ch</u>nology   A. <u>ch</u>icken   B. <u>ch</u>eer   C. <u>ch</u>emistry D. <u>ch</u>air

(　　) 3. tr<u>ea</u>sure   A. dis<u>ea</u>se   B. l<u>ea</u>d   C. br<u>ea</u>the   D. d<u>ea</u>d

(　　) 4. rep<u>or</u>ter   A. p<u>or</u>trait   B. f<u>or</u>get   C. flav<u>or</u>   D. visit<u>or</u>

(　　) 5. v<u>i</u>tality   A. sk<u>i</u>ll   B. dr<u>i</u>ve   C. c<u>i</u>ty   D. art<u>i</u>st

二、英汉互译

1. as early as _____   2. 吸引_____

3. 中国热_____   4. date back to _____

5. search for _____   6. the Olympic Games _____

7. the Silk Road _____ 8. 既不……也不……_____

9. 另外,此外_____   10. 在那时_____

三、用括号内所给汉语提示或单词的适当形式填空

1. He can speak _____ (Spain).
2. What did she _____ (actual) say?
3. The Silk Road was a path of cultural _____ (交流) between the East and the West.
4. Traffic reaches its _____ (顶峰) between 8 and 9 in the morning.
5. He is known as an _____ (art).
6. We should be _____ (好奇的) about the world.
7. The house was built in the 19th _____ (世纪).
8. He told us that the real _____ (财宝) to us was kindness.
9. The movie helped _____ (促进) her screen career.
10. The Silk Road was not just a single _____ (路线).

四、找出下列句子中错误的选项，并改正过来

1. He started writing music as earlier as 1989.
     A   B   C   D

2. I don't believe that the man is killed by Jim, isn't he?
        A   B   C   D

3. He is watching TV at that time.
    A B   C   D

4. could you tell me who were you waiting for?
          A   B   C   D

5. Neither he nor they is totally right.
          A   B   C   D

1.(　　)应为_____　　2.(　　)应为_____　　3.(　　)应为_____
4.(　　)应为_____　　5.(　　)应为_____

单元检测

第一部分　英语知识运用(共分三节，满分40分)

第一节　语音知识：从 A、B、C、D 四个选项中找出其画线部分与所给单词画线部分读音相同的选项。(共 5 分，每小题 1 分)

(　　)1. exhibition　　A. half　　B. homework　　C. hour　　D. handsome

(　　)2. century　　A. lively　　B. fly　　C. why　　D. by

Unit 5　Ancient Civilization

(　　)3. emissary　　A. below　　B. less　　C. exam　　D. reporter
(　　)4. podcast　　A. both　　B. mother　　C. wonderful　　D. coffee
(　　)5. sculpture　　A. pull　　B. but　　C. student　　D. curious

第二节　词汇与语法知识：从 A、B、C、D 四个选项中选出可以填入空白处的最佳选项。(共 25 分，每小题 1 分)

(　　)6. Greece was introduced to silk products from China in _____ 6th century BC.
　　A. the　　B. a　　C. /　　D. that

(　　)7. Everyone was _____ about why Mark was leaving in a hurry.
　　A. relaxed　　B. peaceful　　C. curious　　D. pleased

(　　)8. They are putting up new hotels in order to _____ tourism in this area.
　　A. boost　　B. attract　　C. cause　　D. gain

(　　)9. What the teacher said _____ the students, and everyone was lost in thought.
　　A. annoyed　　B. knocked　　C. enlightened　　D. excited

(　　)10. The two sister cities started a series of sports and cultural _____ with each other last year.
　　A. departments　　B. instructions
　　C. challenges　　D. exchanges

(　　)11. Tomatoes were _____ to China from South America in the Ming Dynasty.
　　A. introduced　　B. avoided　　C. covered　　D. applied

(　　)12. He was nice looking, but I wasn't deeply attracted _____ him.
　　A. at　　B. to　　C. on　　D. in

(　　)13. The police headed to the deep of the mountain in search _____ the lost boy.
　　A. for　　B. from　　C. of　　D. among

(　　)14. Everyone knows that the Silk Road was neither an actual road _____ a single route.
　　A. either　　B. and　　C. or　　D. nor

(　　)15. I don't know _____ the art gallery opens on Tuesdays.
　　A. that　　B. if　　C. when　　D. what

(　　)16. Luxun is famous _____ his great novels.
　　A. as　　B. to　　C. for　　D. in

(　　)17. How long have you prepared _____ this exhibition?
　　A. as　　B. to　　C. for　　D. on

(　　)18. —_____ have you worked in Beijing?
　　—For 5 years.

— 89 —

A. How soon　　B. How often　　C. How long　　D. How far

(　　)19. The students _____ deeply by the teachers every day.

　　A. influence　　　　　　B. influenced

　　C. are influenced　　　　D. were influenced

(　　)20. This overcoat cost too much. _____, they are too small for me.

　　A. What's more　　　　　B. What's new

　　C. What's worse　　　　　D. What's surprise

(　　)21. Not only you but also he _____ wrong.

　　A. is　　　B. are　　　C. were　　　D. am

(　　)22. Of all the geographers, Xu Xiake, _____ me most.

　　A. shocked　　B. impressed　　C. frightened　　D. embarrassed

(　　)23. —Could you please _____ the story _____ French?

　　—No problem.

　　A. translate; with　　　　B. to translate; with

　　C. translate; into　　　　D. to translate; into

(　　)24. The tradition could date back _____ 300BC.

　　A. in　　　B. to　　　C. as　　　D. for

(　　)25. A good way to improve memory is _____ information with pictures.

　　A. link　　B. linked　　C. links　　D. to link

(　　)26. As early as over 2,000 years ago, China and ancient Rome were already connected _____ the Silk Road.

　　A. by　　　B. to　　　C. with　　　D. for

(　　)27. —Do you know _____?

　　—Yes. It usually closes at 9:00 p.m.

　　A. when does the shop close　　B. when the shop closes

　　C. when do the shops close　　　D. when will the shop close

(　　)28. Chinese calligraphy is a traditional art form based on Chinese _____.

　　A. architecture　　B. painting　　C. characters　　D. sculptures

(　　)29. Excuse me. Could you tell me _____ the National Museum is?

　　A. where　　B. how　　C. that　　D. which

(　　)30. —Could you please tell me _____?

　　—Next Thursday morning.

　　A. when we visited the Capital Museum

　　B. when did we visit the Capital Museum

C. when we will visit the Capital Museum

D. when will we visit the Capital Museum

第三节 完形填空：阅读下面的短文，从所给的 **A、B、C、D** 四个选项中选出正确的答案。（共 **10** 分，每小题 **1** 分）

If you want to go somewhere quickly, taking a taxi is the __31__ choice, because it can help you save a lot of time. But there is a strange taxi in __32__. The strange taxi is called the Turtle Taxi. It runs __33__ than other taxis. A Turtle Taxi driver says that he __34__ drives his taxi quickly.

Turtle Taxis are becoming popular in Japan. They are welcomed by the elderly and women with children. They don't like to take a __35__ taxi. They say that the fast taxi makes them feel sick. Many tourists also __36__ Turtle Taxis to travel around the city. They __37__ that it is the best way to travel around __38__ you will have enough time to enjoy the beautiful views on the way.

The drivers of Turtle Taxis drive more slowly and gently(轻柔地). "The starts and stops are very gentle," said a mother with a one-year-old baby. "It is __39__ and __40__ than taking a taxi. My child can have a nice sleep in the car."

( )31. A. bad   B. best   C. good   D. better
( )32. A. Australia   B. America   C. China   D. Japan
( )33. A. lower   B. more slowly   C. slow   D. low
( )34. A. never   B. often   C. always   D. usually
( )35. A. expensive   B. cheap   C. fast   D. slow
( )36. A. ride   B. take   C. lend   D. borrow
( )37. A. talk   B. tell   C. say   D. speak
( )38. A. if   B. but   C. although   D. because
( )39. A. more safe   B. safe   C. dangerous   D. safer
( )40. A. more boring B. boring   C. comfortable   D. more comfortable

第二部分 篇章与词汇理解(共分三节，满分50分)

第一节 阅读理解：阅读下列短文，从每题所给的 **A、B、C、D** 四个选项中，选出最恰当的答案。（共 **30** 分，每小题 **2** 分）

A

A new study shows that, of all the pet owners, almost 77% of them keep dogs as pets, 21% cats, and only 2% rabbits. It is not difficult to find out that in the world of pets, dogs are the most popular ones.

The study says, over 50% of the dog owners describe themselves with the word "hard-working", and about 30% of them say they are "sunny", 20% of them "clean".

How about the cat? Around 21% of the cat owners use the word "shy" to describe themselves, 20% of them "unclean", and 13% of them "lazy". They are really different from dog owners, but they are still cute.

And 56% of the rabbit owners describe themselves "full of new ideas". And 28% of them "long for being free". However, 16% of them are easier to lose their eyes for things.

What's more, rabbit and dog owners say they can get up early, but most cat lovers like to stay up late. And as for the girls and women, the dog owners in the countryside probably have a husband, but the cat owners in their twenties are probably single women.

(　　)41. We can use the words"_____"to describe a cat owner.

  A. sunny but lazy　　　　　B. hard-working and clean

  C. unclean but hard-working　　D. shy and lazy

(　　)42. What do we know about dogs from the passage?

  A. Almost 77% of the world animals are dogs.

  B. As pets, dogs are the most welcomed.

  C. Dogs can work hard for their owners.

  D. Dogs always live in the countryside.

(　　)43. What does the underlined word "single" mean in the last passage?

  A. 单身的　　B. 干练的　　C. 时尚的　　D. 大胆的

(　　)44. Which of the following is TRUE according to the passage?

  A. People should have dogs as pets not cats.

  B. There's no difference between cats and dogs.

  C. It's difficult for some rabbit owners to keep their eyes on one thing.

  D. Both the cat owners and the rabbit owners like staying up late.

(　　)45. What's the best title for this passage?

  A. A Study About What Pets to Keep.

  B. Words to Describe Three Pets.

  C. The Most Popular Pets in the World.

  D. The Owners of Dogs, Cats and Rabbits.

B

To travel around the world is many adventurous (爱冒险的) people's dream. But very few people can afford a global tour because hotels, food and plane tickets are too expensive. Some people, however, have thought of some ways to make their dreams come true.

Laura Cody and Tanbay Theune, a couple from Britain decided to travel around the world. They have found a good way to pay for their trips. They look after pets for rich house owners. In exchange, they can stay in the houses for free. They have looked after houses cows, cats, dogs and fish. In two years, the couple has been to Australia, Germany, Spain and Italy. They have stayed in big cities and small villages. The home owners are usually very generous and have given them food, wine and day trips.

Another person who tries to make her travel dream come true is a photographer, Rhiannon Taylor. She travels around the world to visit, review and take photos of the best hotels. She shares the places where she stays and the food she eats on the Internet with tens of thousands of followers.

With these ways of making money, travelling around the world is no longer a dream. More and more young people are thinking creatively to make their dreams come true.

(　　)46. Why do most people feel hard to make their travel dream come true?
　　　　A. Because it's very difficult for them to find hotels.
　　　　B. Because the food is not healthy.
　　　　C. Because the cost of travel is high.
　　　　D. Because they are afraid of adventure.

(　　)47. Laura and Tanbay paid for their trips by _____.
　　　　A. staying in the house for free
　　　　B. being given food and drinks
　　　　C. going to Australia and other countries
　　　　D. looking after pets for rich house owners

(　　)48. According to the passage, Taylor shares her photos _____.
　　　　A. on the Internet　　　　　　　　B. before her travel
　　　　C. with hundreds of followers　　　D. during staying in hotels

(　　)49. What does the underlined word "generous" mean in Chinese?
　　　　A. 吝啬的　　　B. 友善的　　　C. 慷慨的　　　D. 冷漠的

(　　)50. The best word to describe the way of making the travel dream come true is _____.
　　　　A. special　　　B. creative　　　C. rich　　　D. adventurous

C

Flu(流感) easily spreads from one person to another. If you are weak, you probably catch flu easily. Do you know how you can avoid flu? Here are some suggestions:

Keep in good health

You can eat everything you want but make sure that your diet is healthy. The healthier you are, the better it is for you to avoid any type of illness around. Most doctors suggest drinking lots of fresh fruit juice and water is helpful to avoid flu.

Stay away from people with flu

If a member of a family or a friend has flu, stay away from him/her until he/she is well. Flu is very communicable. If you stay with the person with flu, you can catch flu easily. Wear a mask (罩) and avoid using things that the person with flu is using.

Exercise

Exercising will make you stronger, which means a stronger immune system(免疫系统), too. Exercise often so that your body will keep healthy. It doesn't matter what kind of exercise it is.

Be happy

Happy people are healthy people. Their life isn't stressed out, so they may be safe from illness. If you are unhappy, you will easily get sick.

Avoiding the flu is easy. Just strength(加强) your immune system and it will take care of the rest.

( )51. How many suggestions are talked about in the passage?

  A. Three.   B. Four.   C. Five.   D. Six.

( )52. The underlined word "communicable" means "_____".

  A. 有效的   B. 无效的   C. 致命的   D. 传染的

( )53. What should we do to stay away from people with flu?

  A. Exercise often.   B. Eat junk food.

  C. Be happy.   D. Wear a mask.

( )54. The passage tells us that _____ can't keep us healthy.

  A. drinking fruit juice and water

  B. exercising

  C. being unhappy

  D. stay away from people with flu

( )55. What's the best title for the passage?

  A. How to avoid flu.   B. How to keep in good health.

  C. How to exercise.   D. How to be happy.

第二节 词义搭配：从(B)栏中选出(A)栏单词的正确解释。(共**10**分，每小题**1**分)

    (A)   (B)

( )56. century   A. a way for travel or transportation

( )57. exchange   B. full of life and energy

( )58. indeed   C. something that is remembered

Unit 5　Ancient Civilization

(　)59. route　　　　D. a painting of a person's face

(　)60. link　　　　E. the highest point

(　)61. reporter　　F. in truth

(　)62. peak　　　　G. a period of 100 years

(　)63. lively　　　H. a person who reports news

(　)64. portrait　　I. the act of changing one thing for another thing

(　)65. memory　　　J. connect or put together two or more pieces

第三节　补全对话：根据对话内容，从对话后的选项中选出能填入空白处的最佳选项。(共10分，每小题2分)

J：Have you watched the TV show *The Ancient Treasures*?

S：Oh, yes. __66__ We are attracted to it quite a lot.

J：The ancient artifacts in the program are extremely amazing. __67__

S：Me too. It is reported that some of the artifacts are on display at the National Museum. __68__

J：Wow! That's cool. Why not go there this afternoon?

S：Well, __69__

J：Let's go and find out. __70__

S：All right. Now let's find a restaurant and have lunch first.

> A. I don't know if the museum opens on Mondays.
> B. My parents and I watch the program every Friday.
> C. Perhaps we can pay a visit there.
> D. Anyway, it's only ten minutes' walk.
> E. I hope that I can admire them in person.

第三部分　语言技能应用(共分四节，满分30分)

第一节　单词拼写：根据下列句子及所给汉语注释，在相应题号后的横线上写出该单词的正确形式。(共5分，每小题1分)

71. We want to introduce the latest _____(技术)into schools.

72. At the age of 70, he is still full of _____(活力).

73. One day, a rich man asked me to paint a _____(画像) for him.

74. The book will _____(启迪)the reader.

75. It was full of colours and special _____(文字).

第二节　词形变换：用括号内单词的适当形式填空。(共5分，每小题1分)

76. A group of _____(report) followed her.

77. Zheng He was a famous _____ (explore).

78. His _____ (exhibit) opens on February 5.

79. Picasso was a Spanish _____ (sculpture).

80. _____ (culture) exchanges are a way of building bridges between countries.

第三节　改错：从 A、B、C、D 四个画线处找出一处错误的选项，填入括号内，并在横线上写出正确答案。(共 10 分，每小题 2 分)

81. I <u>can</u> use the computer <u>to</u> play <u>games</u> and search <u>of</u> some useful information.
　　　A　　　　　　　　　　B　　　　C　　　　　　　D

82. The Great Wall <u>is</u> one of <u>the world's</u> <u>most</u> famous <u>wonder</u>.
　　　　　　　　A　　　　　B　　　　C　　　　　　D

83. Which <u>artist</u> or works <u>impresses</u> you <u>most</u> <u>in</u> the exhibition?
　　　　　A　　　　　　　B　　　　　　C　　D

84. The <u>teacher</u> told <u>us</u> <u>that</u> the earth <u>was</u> round.
　　　　　A　　　　B　　C　　　　　　D

85. This letter <u>will</u> be <u>send</u> <u>to</u> <u>England</u>.
　　　　　　　　A　　　　B　　C　　D

81.(　　) 应为 _____　　82.(　　) 应为 _____　　83.(　　) 应为 _____

84.(　　) 应为 _____　　85.(　　) 应为 _____

第四节　书面表达。(共 10 分)

作文题目：The Silk Road

词数要求：80~100 词

写作要点：1. 丝绸之路有着悠久的历史；
　　　　　2. 丝绸之路发挥了巨大作用。

Unit 6

Craftsmanship

Warming-up

一、句型汇总

1. What qualities do you think a fashion designer should have? 你认为时装设计师应该有什么样的品质?

2. As a watchmaker, he should be hard-working and persistent. 作为一个钟表匠,他应该是勤劳的和坚持不懈的。

3. He always tries his best to finish his work. 他总是竭尽全力地完成他的工作。

4. Every watch is designed, made and assembled here. 每块手表都是在这儿被设计、制作和组装的。

5. The watchmakers need to focus on every small detail in the whole process. 制表师需要关注整个过程中的每一个细节。

6. Swiss watches are always connected to an impressive number of new watch making skills and patents. 瑞士手表总是与数量惊人的新型制表技能和专利联系到一起的。

7. When I first took up the work, what I saw was the whole of ox. 当我第一次从事这项工作时,我所看到的是整头牛。

8. The advantage of Japanese production lies in continued learning and creating. 日本产品的

优势在于连续不断地学习和创造。

9. The high quality of the products depends largely on the craftsman spirit of German people. 产品的高质量在很大程度上取决于德国人民的工匠精神。

10. Chinese people still carry forward craftsmanship and strive for excellence. 中国人依然发扬工匠精神,精益求精。

二、英汉互译

1. carving wood _____   2. quality _____
3. welding steel _____   4. design _____
5. watchmaker _____   6. 创造性的_____
7. 坚持不懈的_____   8. 技术,工艺_____
9. 热心肠_____   10. 勤劳的_____

Listening and Speaking

一、找出与所给单词画线部分读音相同的选项

( ) 1. a̲chieve   A. a̲gency   B. a̲ctually   C. a̲ctive   D. a̲ssemble

( ) 2. spee̲ch   A. but̲cher   B. te̲chnology   C. heada̲che   D. stoma̲ch

( ) 3. continue̲d   A. helpe̲d   B. staye̲d   C. wante̲d   D. worke̲d

( ) 4. gra̲ceful   A. ca̲re   B. sta̲ndard   C. pa̲tience   D. pa̲tent

( ) 5. we̲ld   A. a̲ssemble   B. de̲velop   C. pre̲pare   D. re̲sult

二、情景交际的单项选择题

( ) 1. —Would you do me a favor and carry these books?
—_____
A. Yes, that's right   B. No trouble
C. Never mind   D. With pleasure

( ) 2. —I can't go with you today, There will be a test tomorrow.
—_____. Maybe next time.
A. It doesn't matter   B. My pleasure
C. I don't think so   D. Sorry to hear that

( )3. —I can't find my watch.

　　　—you _____ it in your office.

　　　A. must have forgotten　　　B. must have left

　　　C. must leave　　　D. must forget

( )4. —When did the computer crash?

　　　—This morning, while I _____ the reading materials downloaded from some websites.

　　　A. have sorted　　B. was sorting　　C. am sorting　　D. had sorted

( )5. I wonder if I could possibly use your bike for tonight? _____. I'm not using it anyhow.

　　　A. Sure, go ahead　　　B. I don't know

　　　C. Yes, indeed　　　D. I don't care

三、用所给句子补全下面对话

A：Hi, lily! What are you doing?

B： 1

A：Well. What is it about then?

B： 2

A：You must be talking about those Chinese famous craftsmen.

B：Actually, I want to introduce some ordinary people in our daily life. 3

A：You are right. 4

B：They should be hard-working and warm-hearted.

A： 5

B：It will take me about six minutes to finish it.

A：Wish you a great success!

B：Thank you.

> A. Like teachers, nurses and welders.
> B. Preparing an English speech for tomorrow's speech contest.
> C. It's about the spirit of craftsmanship.
> D. How long will it take you to finish it?
> E. What are they like?

四、场景模拟

编写一组对话, 向你的同学介绍 Chinese famous craftsmen。

提示词汇: good quality; an expert; hard-working; be patient; be creative; persistent; try one's best; to strive for perfection

Reading and Writing

一、用括号内所给汉语提示或单词的适当形式填空

1. A speech contest on _____ (大国工匠) will be held in our school tomorrow.

2. The man was asked to _____ (宰杀) a pig last week.

3. John is a maintenance worker and know how to fix electrical _____ (设备).

4. He is _____ (准备) for the interview.

5. The income and the living _____ (水平,标准) of workers are rising.

6. Nothing is a waste if you have a _____ (create) mind.

7. In my opinion, the young like _____ (fashion) things.

8. Playing chess cultivated(培养) my _____ (patient) and perseverance.

9. It is an impressive _____ (achieve).

10. The fashion designer is serious and strive for _____ (perfect).

二、完形填空

Who designed the first helicopter(直升机)? Who __1__ the most famous pictures in the world? Who knew more about the human body than most __2__. There is an answer __3__ all these questions-Leonardo de Vinci.

Leonardo may have been the greatest genius __4__ have ever known. He lived in Italy around the year 1,500, but many of his inventions seem modern to us today. For example, one of his notebooks has drawings of a helicopter. Of course, he couldn't __5__ a helicopter with the thing he had. But scientists say his idea would have worked.

But Leonardo __6__ an inventor. He was one of the greatest artists of his day. By the time he was twenty years old, he was called a master painter, and as he got older he became __7__ more famous. Sometimes he drew a hand ten different ways __8__ he was ready to paint.

Many of Leonardo's wonderful paintings are still with __9__ today. You may know one of his most famous works the __10__ woman known as the Mona Lisa.

( ) 1. A. took　　　　　B. made　　　　　C. painted　　　　D. invented
( ) 2. A. artists　　　　B. doctors　　　　C. painters　　　　D. people
( ) 3. A. to　　　　　　B. of　　　　　　　C. for　　　　　　D. from
( ) 4. A. the scientists　B. the artists　　　C. the world　　　D. people
( ) 5. A. draw　　　　　B. paint　　　　　　C. work　　　　　D. build
( ) 6. A. was just　　　 B. wasn't just　　　C. wasn't　　　　　D. was no longer
( ) 7. A. less　　　　　B. no　　　　　　　C. even　　　　　　D. very
( ) 8. A. before　　　　B. after　　　　　　C. because　　　　D. when
( ) 9. A. him　　　　　B. us　　　　　　　C. them　　　　　　D. you
( ) 10. A. interesting　　B. crying　　　　　C. smiling　　　　　D. surprising

三、阅读理解

阅读下面短文,从每题所给的 A、B、C、D 四个选项中选出最佳答案。

There was a man who had two children, a boy and a girl. The boy was good-looking but the girl was not. One day they found a mirror for the first time and they saw what they looked like. The boy was very pleased and he said to his sister, "How handsome I am! I look much nicer than you!" The girl did not like what her brother said and gave him a hard push(推). "Go away!" she said. Their father saw what was happening. He went up to them and said to the boy, "You must always be good as well as look good." Then to the girl he said, "My dear, if you help everyone and do your best to please him, everyone will love you. It does not matter that you are not as good-looking as your brother."

( ) 1. A man had _____.

　　A. a good-looking boy

　　B. an ugly girl

　　C. two good-looking children

　　D. a boy and a girl

( ) 2. The boy saw what he looked like in the mirror and was happy because he _____.

　　A. found a mirror

B. knew he looked as nice as his sister

C. and his sister were good-looking

D. was handsome

( )3. The girl gave the boy a hard push because _____.

A. she was stronger

B. what he said was wrong

C. she was not happy about what he said

D. her farther loved her

( )4. The father told the girl that _____.

A. it was important to be good-looking

B. it was a good thing to be ugly

C. if she helps people, everyone will love her

D. she was as good-looking as her brother

( )5. Which one is NOT mentioned in the text?

A. The man.　　B. The mum.　　C. The boy.　　D. The girl.

四、书面表达

以"The spirit of craftsman"为题，写一篇文章，词数为 80~100 词。

写作要点：1. 什么是工匠精神？（精雕细琢，追求完美，咫尺匠心难，成大事不在于力的大小，而在于能坚持多久，一心一意，坚持不懈地做好每一件事）

2. 弘扬工匠精神（精益求精、追求卓越、爱岗敬业、勤劳苦干等品格）

3. 谈谈作为中职生，我们应该怎么做。（好品质、勤奋学习）

Grammar

一、从下面每小题四个选项中选出最佳选项

(   ) 1. After school we went to the reading room, only to be told that it _____.
   A. was decorated   B. had decorated
   C. had been decorating   D. was being decorated

(   ) 2. Our friendship _____ quickly over the weeks that followed.
   A. had developed   B. was developing
   C. would develop   D. developed

(   ) 3. This new building _____ our school.
   A. is belong to   B. belongs to   C. belongs for   D. belongs to

(   ) 4. The flowers were so lovely that they _____ in no time.
   A. sold   B. had been sold   C. were sold   D. would sell

(   ) 5. Our library _____ in 1991.
   A. builds   B. built   C. is built   D. was built

(   ) 6. These books _____ by my friend for a week.
   A. have kept   B. were kept   C. have been kept   D. had kept

(   ) 7. The garden requires _____ every week
   A. to water   B. to be watered   C. watered   D. water

(   ) 8. The pen _____ smoothly.
   A. writes   B. write   C. is written   D. wrote

(   ) 9. The teacher could not make himself _____ because the students were so noisy.
   A. pay attention   B. paid attention to
   C. paid attention   D. to be paid attention to

(   ) 10. It was said that a new robot _____ next year.
   A. designed   B. has been designed
   C. would be designed   D. will design

(   ) 11. This kind of cloth _____ well and _____ long.
   A. is washed; lasted   B. washes; lasts
   C. washes; is lasted   D. washed; lasted

(　　)12. _____ a new dormitory _____ in our school last year?

　　A. Is; built　　　　　　　　B. Was; built

　　C. Does; build　　　　　　　D. Did; build

(　　)13. Our teacher _____ carefully.

　　A. should be listened　　　　B. should listen

　　C. be listened　　　　　　　D. is listened

(　　)14. As we know, all the rules in school _____.

　　A. must keep to　　　　　　B. must be kept

　　C. must keep　　　　　　　D. must be kept up

(　　)15. The little girl is seen _____ to hospital.

　　A. to take　　B. to taken　　C. to be taken　　D. be taken

(　　)16. —Have you moved into your new building?

　　—No yet. The rooms _____.

　　A. are being painted　　　　B. are painting

　　C. Are painted　　　　　　　D. are having painted

(　　)17. The new bridge _____ by the end of last month.

　　A. has been designed　　　　B. had been designed

　　C. was design　　　　　　　D. would be designed

(　　)18. Don't litter everywhere. Look at the sign: "rubbish _____ into the dustbin."

　　A. has thrown　　B. was thrown　　C. must throw　　D. must be thrown

(　　)19. John will call his father for help when his car needs _____.

　　A. to repair　　B. repairing　　C. being repaired　　D. be repaired

(　　)20. Great changes have taken place in the city and a lot of factories _____.

　　A. have been set up　　　　B. was set up

　　C. have set up　　　　　　　D. set up

(　　)21. You can't move in right now. the house _____ now.

　　A. has painted　　　　　　B. is painted

　　C. is being painted　　　　D. is painting

(　　)22. They have had a good start, but more work needs _____ to achieve the final success.

　　A. Being done　　B. do　　C. to be done　　D. to do

(　　)23. —Have you finished your project?

　　—Not yet, I'll finish if I _____ ten more minutes.

　　A. give　　　　B. am given　　　C. have given　　　D. will be given

(　　)24. The classroom _____ by students every day.
　　　　A. should clean　　　　　　B. are cleaned
　　　　C. should be cleaned　　　　D. is cleaning

(　　)25. I promise that your children will _____ while you are away.
　　　　A. take care　　　　　　　B. take care of
　　　　C. be taken care of　　　　D. be taken care

(　　)26. Who _____ to Canada next year?
　　　　A. will be sent　　　　　　B. will send
　　　　C. is going to send　　　　D. are going to send

(　　)27. A new government _____ after the war.
　　　　A. set up　　B. put up　　C. was set up　　D. built

(　　)28. Quality _____ the life of product.
　　　　A. regards as　　　　　　B. is regarded as
　　　　C. regarded as　　　　　　D. regards to

(　　)29. I will need more than one hour before my homework _____.
　　　　A. has completed　　　　　B. has been completed
　　　　C. is completed　　　　　　D. completes

(　　)30. His complaint _____ in two days.
　　　　A. is dealt with　　　　　　B. will deal with
　　　　C. has been dealt with　　　D. will be dealt with

二、找出下列句子中错误的选项，并改正过来

1. I told the sports meeting would be held in three days.
　　A　　B　　　　　　　C　　　D

2. Those flowers on the desk are looked beautiful, don't they?
　　　　　　A　　　　B　　　C　　　　　　D

3. The sports meeting will be taken place on the playground next week.
　　A　　　　　　B　　　C　　　　　D

4. A new building will built in our school next year.
　　A　　B　　　C　　　　　D

5. The flowers require to watering.
　　A　　B　　C　　D

6. The worker said that some factories are being built in her hometown.
　　　　　　A　　B　　　　　　　　C　　　D

7. My mother told me don't to play in the street.
　　　　　　A　　B　　C　　D

8. I was amazing at her skill and patience.
　　　A　　B　　　　C　　D

9. He was made play football on the playground.
      A   B   C   D

10. The silk dress is felt very soft.
    A   B C D

1.(　) 应为_____　　2.(　) 应为_____　　3.(　) 应为_____
4.(　) 应为_____　　5.(　) 应为_____　　6.(　) 应为_____
7.(　) 应为_____　　8.(　) 应为_____　　9.(　) 应为_____
10.(　) 应为_____

For Better Performance

一、找出与所给单词画线部分读音相同的选项

(　)1. craft   A. continued   B. cent   C. recently   D. cinema

(　)2. persistent   A. enlighten   B. prize   C. assistant   D. strive

(　)3. pleasure   A. measure   B. creative   C. beach   D. feature

(　)4. excellence A. exhibit   B. explain   C. exactly   D. expert

(　)5. exactly   A. type   B. spy   C. memory   D. fly

二、英汉互译

1. once upon a time _____　　2. neither...nor _____

3. in the end _____　　4. be regarded as _____

5. care for _____　　6. 与……有联系 _____

7. 集中于 _____　　8. 从事；拿起 _____

9. 争取；奋斗 _____　　10. 代代相传 _____

三、用括号内所给单词的适当形式填空

1. His _____ (achieve) is astonishing and this book is the jewel in his crown.

2. Our teachers are always _____ (friend) to all of us.

3. She was _____ (disappoint) when she saw the result.

4. The expert is finding _____ (create) ways to make a change.

5. She has always wanted to a fashion _____ (design).

6. It is of great _____ (important) for us to study English.

7. The advantage of Japanese _____ (produce) lies in learning and creating.

8. She often wears a _____ (fashion) hat.

9. Creation and _____ (patient) are very important in making kites.

10. Chinese people still carry forward craftsmanship and strive for _____ (excellent).

四、找出下列句子中错误的选项，并改正过来

1. It is said that he used to spend five hours swim in the river.
　　A　　　　B　　　　　　　C　　　　　　　D

2. The advantage of production lies in continue learning and creating.
　　　　A　　　　　　　　B　　　　C　　　　　　　　　D

3. Products made in Germany believed to be well-built and durable.
　　A　　　B　　　　　　　　C　　　　　　D

4. It was such funny story that we all like it.
　　　　　A　　B　　　C　　　　D

5. The problem being discussed at the meeting is of great important.
　　　　　　　A　　　B　　　　　C　　　　　　　D

1.(　　) 应为_____　　2.(　　) 应为_____　　3.(　　) 应为_____

4.(　　) 应为_____　　5.(　　) 应为_____

单元检测

第一部分　英语知识运用(共分三节，满分40分)

第一节　语音知识：从 A、B、C、D 四个选项中找出其画线部分与所给单词画线部分读音相同的选项。(共5分，每小题1分)

(　) 1. patience　　A. dynasty　　B. famous　　C. suitable　　D. comfortable

(　) 2. honor　　A. hour　　B. happy　　C. hotel　　D. behind

(　) 3. focus　　A. colleague　　B. production　　C. collect　　D. program

(　) 4. practice　　A. city　　B. craftsmanship　　C. concern　　D. reception

(　) 5. continued　　A. supply　　B. future　　C. butcher　　D. include

第二节　词汇与语法知识：从 A、B、C、D 四个选项中选出可以填入空白处的最佳选项。(共25分，每小题1分)

(　) 6. Every year many people _____ diseases _____ pollution.

　　A. die from; related　　　　B. die of; relate

　　C. die of; related to　　　　D. die from; relating

(   )7. The worker said that some new workshops _____ in his hometown now.
   A. are building　　　　　　　　　B. have been built
   C. are being built　　　　　　　　D. were being built

(   )8. _____ Tom, Jane got married last month.
   A. According to　　　　　　　　　B. According for
   C. According in　　　　　　　　　D. According

(   )9. Ann didn't attend the meeting yesterday. She _____ be ill.
   A. can　　　　B. may　　　　C. should　　　　D. must

(   )10. His answer was so _____ that we were _____ and didn't know what to say.
   A. amazing; amazed　　　　　　　B. amazing; amazing
   C. amazed; amazing　　　　　　　D. amazed; amazed

(   )11. My bike is broken. It needs _____.
   A. to repair　　B. repairing　　C. repaired　　D. be repaired

(   )12. Every possible means _____ to prevent the pollution, but the sky is still not clear.
   A. is used　　　　　　　　　　　B. are used
   C. has been used　　　　　　　　D. have been used

(   )13. —Do you like the coat?
   　　—It _____ soft.
   A. is feeling　　B. felt　　C. feels　　D. is felt

(   )14. Xi'an is _____ that we are all struck by the beauty of it.
   A. such ancient a city　　　　　　B. such a ancient city
   C. so ancient a city　　　　　　　D. so an ancient city

(   )15. A kind of serious disease _____ in the world last year.
   A. broke out　　　　　　　　　　B. break out
   C. was broken out　　　　　　　　D. has been broken out

(   )16. Dr. Zhong Nanshan is famous _____ a medical scientist.
   A. to　　　　B. as　　　　C. for　　　　D. with

(   )17. Is _____ necessary to tell his father everything?
   A. it　　　　B. that　　　　C. what　　　　D. he

(   )18. The meeting which _____ tomorrow is of great importance.
   A. will be held　　　　　　　　　B. will hold
   C. is going to hold　　　　　　　　D. held

Unit 6　Craftsmanship

(　　)19. _____ I know, he has been here for half a year.
　　A. As long as　　B. As far as　　C. As well as　　D. As soon as

(　　)20. _____ useful information you bring here!
　　A. What　　B. What a　　C. How　　D. How a

(　　)21. It is impossible to _____ one's goal without working hard.
　　A. achieve　　B. get　　C. arrive　　D. make

(　　)22. Neither the students nor the teacher _____ smoke here.
　　A. allows　　B. is allowed　　C. allow　　D. are allowed

(　　)23. I don't think _____ possible _____ us to solve all the problems.
　　A. it; for　　B. that; of　　C. it; of　　D. that; for

(　　)24. Every day, he goes to work by bus _____ his car.
　　A. instead driving
　　B. instead of drive
　　C. instead of driving
　　D. Instead to drive

(　　)25. Our teacher asked us to spend more time _____ English every day.
　　A. to practice speaking
　　B. practicing speaking
　　C. to practice to speak
　　D. practicing to speak

(　　)26. The old man _____ by nurse in the hospital now.
　　A. take care of
　　B. is taking care of
　　C. is being taken care of
　　D. is taken care of

(　　)27. I believe that his experience is enough to _____ this job.
　　A. take off　　B. take up　　C. take place　　D. take in

(　　)28. She was _____, and _____ the sick in hospital.
　　A. determined; care for
　　B. determined; cared for
　　C. determination; cared for
　　D. determined; cared with

(　　)29. Whether we will go camping tomorrow _____ the weather.
　　A. depend on　　B. depends on　　C. depending on　　D. is depended on

(　　)30. You need to _____ every details when carving a picture on stone.
　　A. focus on　　B. carry on　　C. come on　　D. agree on

第三节　完形填空：阅读下面的短文，从所给的 A、B、C、D 四个选项中选出正确的答案。（共 10 分，每小题 1 分）

　　A twenty-year-old immigrant Levi Strauss, ___31___ to the United States in 1850. This man made his fortune on canvas that he found good for working clothes. In the past, only poor men ___32___ jeans. ___33___ were worn by miners, truck drivers, farmers and factory workers. Today, jeans are no longer looked down upon. They are worn by both men ___34___ women, by both skilled and unskilled workers, __35__ both employees and employers.

Because everyone can __36__ comfortable in them, the blue-jeans invented for the use of workers __37__ now almost everywhere, anytime. This is true not only in the United States, __38__ in many other countries in the world. Although unable to __39__ the same language, the inhabitants earth have at least agreed to wear the same pants. Jeans are becoming more and __40__ popular today.

( )31. A. come   B. came   C. coming   D. has come
( )32. A. wear   B. wearing   C. worn   D. wore
( )33. A. Jeans   B. They   C. Canvas   D. Clothes
( )34. A. and   B. both   C. two   D. or
( )35. A. on   B. in   C. by   D. with
( )36. A. do   B. is   C. feel   D. enjoy
( )37. A. are   B. is   C. be   D. became
( )38. A. so   B. but also   C. too   D. as well
( )39. A. speak   B. say   C. tell   D. express
( )40. A. much   B. less   C. many   D. more

第二部分　篇章与词汇理解(共分三节，满分50分)

第一节　阅读理解：阅读下列短文，从每题所给的A、B、C、D四个选项中，选出最恰当的答案。(共30分，每小题2分)

A

Be honest. That's all you have to do on Honesty Day. It would be great if we were all honest every day of the year. It's good that there is a day to encourage honesty. M. Hirsh started Honesty Day. He chose the last day of April because the first day is April Fool's Day. which celebrates lies, on Honesty Day, anyone may ask you any questions and you should give a true and honest answer. That means that you have knowledge of Honesty Day.

M. Hirsh wrote a book on telling lies. He said in his book that almost all people lie about 200 times a day. In our daily life, a typical lie for a man is "I didn't drink that much " and for a woman is "Nothing is wrong. I'm fine." It is found that nurses are the most honest people, while sales people and politicians(政客) are the biggest liars.

Every Honest Day, M. Hirsh hands out prizes to honest people.

( )41. Which of the following is Honesty Day?
　　A. April 1st　　B. April 10th.　　C. April 20th.　　D. April 30th.

( )42. The underlined word in Paragraph 2 possibly means _____.
   A. 诚实的人   B. 说谎的人   C. 领导人   D. 统治者

( )43. What should people do on Honest Day?
   A. Tell the truth only.   B. Tell lies only.
   C. Tell the truth or tell lies.   D. Keep silent.

( )44. According to the passage, _____ are the most honest people.
   A. salesman   B. politicians   C. nurses   D. all people

( )45. M. Hirsh started Honesty Day to _____.
   A. hand out prizes   B. answer questions
   C. encourage honesty   D. celebrate lies

B

When Susan Chen left high school, she wanted to go to university. Unfortunately, her family was quite poor, and a university education cost a lot of money.

"Take the entrance examination," her father said, "and I Will try to support you if you pass."

Susan took the examination. She did not score very high marks, but she scored enough. And she was offered a place at the university.

"I'm very proud of you, Susan." her father said, "I must find the money for you somehow. I will sell my car and work at two jobs if necessary because I think your future is worth the Sacrifice." "You are a great father, dad" Susan said. The next day he sold his car and asked his boss to give him 3 hours over time every day. He was very tired, but he never complained.

A year passed, Susan passed her first-year examination and got the third place, and won thes cholarship.

She told his father, "You can have your car and stop working."

( )46. Susan wanted to _____ when she graduated from high school?
   A. make some money   B. go to university
   C. go abroad   D. go to work

( )47. She took the entrance examination and passed it with _____.
   A. full marks   B. the highest marks
   C. the lowest marks   D. just enough marks

( )48. To pay for her university education, her father _____.
   A. sold his house and furniture
   B. change his job and worked hard
   C. sold his car and worked more time

D. give her his car and a lot of money

( )49. At the end of her first year at the university, Susan _____.

A. passed the exam and won the scholarship

B. failed the exam and was fired

C. passed the exam but didn't win the scholarship

D. bought his father a car and gave him much money

( )50. From the story, we can see it is probably true that _____.

A. Susan didn't work hard at her study at university

B. Susan found a job to have her father's car back

C. Mr.Chen was pleased to hear the news from his daughter

D. Susan earned much money by working for his father

C

Paper is one of the most important products ever invented by man. The invention of paper meant that more people could be educated because more books could be printed. Paper provided an important way to communicate with knowledge.

Paper was first made in China about 2,000 years ago. In Egypt and the West, paper was not very commonly used before the year 1,400. Paper was not made in southern Europe until about the year 1,100. After that the foreign countries of Canada, Sweden, Norway, Finland, and the United States became the most important in paper making. Today Finland makes the best paper in the world. And it has the biggest paper industry in the world.

When we think of paper, we think of newspapers, books, letters, and writing paper. So paper plays an important role in our lives. Paper is very good for keeping you warm. Houses are often insulated (隔热的) with paper. You have perhaps seen homeless men sleep on a large number of newspapers. They are insulating themselves from the cold. In Finland, in winter it is sometimes 40℃ below zero. The farmers wear paper boots in the snow. <u>Nothing could be warmer.</u>

( )51. What did the invention of paper mean?

A. It meant more people could be educated.

B. It meant more books could be printed.

C. It meant paper is one of the most important products.

D. It meant paper was invented by man.

( )52. When was paper made in southern Europe?

A. Before 1,100.   B. After 1,400.

C. After 1,100.   D. Before 1,400.

( )53. Which country makes the best paper today?
　　A. Norway.　　　　　　　　B. Canada.
　　C. The United States.　　　D. Finland.

( )54. What's the meaning of the underlined sentence "Nothing could be warmer"?
　　A. Books are warmer.　　　B. Newspapers are warmer.
　　C. Paper is the warmest.　　D. Houses are the warmest.

( )55. What's the main idea of the passage?
　　A. The invention of paper.　B. The best paper.
　　C. The paper-making.　　　D. The uses of paper.

第二节　词义搭配：从(B)栏中选出(A)栏单词的正确解释。（共10分，每小题1分）

　　　　　(A)　　　　　　　　　(B)

( )56. speech　　　A. the act of doing something
( )57. instead　　　B. to join one thing to another
( )58. practice　　　C. unlike anything else
( )59. ordinary　　　D. a level by which someone is judged
( )60. unique　　　E. go on doing something
( )61. standard　　　F. a formal talk
( )62. amazing　　　G. take the place of, replace
( )63. achieve　　　H. astonishing
( )64. continue　　　I. gain
( )65. connect　　　J. common, usual

第三节　补全对话：根据对话内容，从对话后的选项中选出能填入空白处的最佳选项。（共10分，每小题2分）

A：Good morning, Lily!
B：Morning! ___66___
A：Yeah, I got the third place.
B：___67___ It's really hard work to prepair for an English Writing Contest.
A：Yeah, and sometimes I even wanted to give up.
B：___68___ And you won in the end.
A：I'd like to thank you for help.
B：How about a celebration?
A：Right! ___69___
B：We have dinner together first and then go hiking.
A：___70___

A. How would you like to celebrate?
B. Congratulations!
C. I've heard you got a prize in the English Writing Contest.
D. Fantastic! Let's go.
E. But you didn't.

第三部分　语言技能应用(共分四节,满分30分)

第一节　单词拼写:根据下列句子及所给汉语注释,在相应题号后的横线上写出该单词的正确形式。(共5分,每小题1分)

71. He has an _____(令人惊异的) attitude toward life.

72. Johnson doesn't look _____(优雅的), but he sure is powerful.

73. What _____(品质) do you think a watchmaker have?

74. Her performance was pretty _____(令人印象深刻的).

75. As a watchmaker, he should be hard-working and _____(坚持不懈的).

第二节　词形变换:用括号内单词的适当形式填空。(共5分,每小题1分)

76. She didn't do enough _____(prepare) for his exam.

77. It was hard work, but the sense of _____(achieve) is huge.

78. They were watching her every _____(move).

79. Lives are no _____(different), there are two sides to everything.

80. The _____(important) of washing hands before a meal is known to everyone.

第三节　改错:从A、B、C、D四个画线处找出一处错误的选项,填入括号内,并在横线上写出正确答案。(共10分,每小题2分)

81. It was so a beautiful day that we all went out for a walk.
　　　A B　　　　　　　　　C　　　　　　　D

82. Whom do you think is the best doctor in the hospital?
　　A　　B　　　　C　　D

83. Our teachers always ask us don't to be late for school.
　　　　　　　　　　A　　B　C　　　D

84. A new building is planning by the engineer now.
　　A　　B　　　　C　　　　D

85. What a great progress they have made in their English.
　　　A　　B　　　　C　　D

81.(　)应为_____　82.(　)应为_____　83.(　)应为_____
84.(　)应为_____　85.(　)应为_____

第四节 书面表达。(共 10 分)

作文题目：My dream

词数要求：80~100 词

写作要点：1. 说说什么是梦想；

             2. 谈谈你自己的梦想；

             3. 说说如何实现你的梦想。

Unit 7

Invention and Innovation

Warming-up

一、句型汇总

1. What kind of high-tech products or software do you often use in your daily life? 你在日常生活中经常使用什么高科技产品或软件？

2. What would life be like without Wi-Fi? 没有无线网的生活将是什么样的呢？

二、英汉互译

1. bluetooth _____
2. 无人机 _____
3. Wi-Fi _____
4. 智能手表 _____
5. 3D printer _____
6. 虚拟现实 _____
7. Internet _____
8. 电脑 _____
9. invention _____
10. 创新 _____

Listening and Speaking

一、找出与所给单词画线部分读音相同的选项

( ) 1. b<u>e</u>nefit   A. activ<u>e</u>   B. ag<u>e</u>ncy   C. <u>e</u>thnic   D. <u>e</u>ventually

( ) 2. b<u>e</u>sides   A. h<u>a</u>rdship   B. <u>o</u>ption   C. s<u>e</u>ction   D. s<u>i</u>gn

( ) 3. dr<u>o</u>ne   A. dev<u>o</u>tion   B. d<u>o</u>uble   C. pr<u>o</u>duct   D. ge<u>o</u>grapher

( ) 4. f<u>ea</u>ture   A. s<u>ea</u>rch   B. b<u>ea</u>ch   C. cr<u>ea</u>tive   D. disapp<u>ea</u>r

( ) 5. f<u>u</u>nction   A. s<u>u</u>ffer   B. q<u>u</u>it   C. <u>u</u>nique   D. act<u>u</u>ally

二、从(B)栏中找出与(A)栏中相对应的答语

(A)

1. What do you recommend?
2. What do you think of it?
3. How is it selling?
4. What's the function of this product?
5. Is it easy to operate?

(B)

A. It can break down food.
B. I's well received by customers.
C. Of course. Just give it a voice command and it will do as you say.
D. What about this one?
E. It is good in quality and cheap in price.

三、用所给句子补全下面对话

A: Hello, Mr. Brown. I know you're writing a book. Can I ask you some questions about it?

B: Sure.

A: 1

B: It's about life in the future.

A: Oh, it must be interesting. What do you think of the life in the future? Will people still use money?

B: No, they won't. Everything will be free then.

A: That's great. What about kids?   2

B: No, they won't. They will study at home on computers.

A: 3

B: Yes, they will have robots at home. Robots will be very common.

A: Oh, life will be exiting in the future. __4__

B: It'll come out next year.

A: Oh. __5__

> A. What's your book about?
> B. I can't wait to read it.
> C. Will they have to go to school?
> D. When will it come out?
> E. Will they have robots at home?

四、场景模拟

编写一组对话，一位导购向顾客介绍医用机器人。

提示词汇：medical robot; quality; price; latest; function; distribute medicine; medical operations.

_____

_____

_____

_____

_____

_____

Reading and Writing

一、用括号内所给汉语提示或单词的适当形式填空

1. _____（科技）has left a mark on our lives.

2. In the beginning, people were _____ (doubt) about spending money on a product without seeing it face to face.

3. Every person is _____ (surround) by technology in a way.

4. It _____ (allow) you to lock the doors of your entire house by making a few clicks.

5. Besides making life easier, it is promoting a _____（严密保护的）environment at home.

6. Innovations are _____ (benefit) almost every industry while changing the way things

work.

7. The future is all about robots, smart homes and _____(无人驾驶的) cars.

8. _____(线上的) shopping is very popular among people now.

9. There are all kinds of information on the _____(网络).

10. _____(智能的) phones have become a part of daily life for more and more people.

二、完形填空

In ancient times, the Four Great Inventions in China had a great influence on the whole world. In recent years, China once again has __1__ its ability to change the world with its "four great new Inventions": high-speed railways, mobile payment, bike-sharing and online shopping.

Do you know __2__ the new inventions can appear in China? The "four great new inventions" are __3__ related to China's high-tech innovation. For example, the operating mode of bike sharing is based __4__ the satellite navigation system (卫星导航系统) mobile payment, big data and other high technologies. This shows that China's high-tech innovation has greatly __5__ the quality of people's lives.

China has entered a new innovative era, thanks to the large amount of __6__ that China has spent encouraging innovation. China is beginning to lead in innovation __7__ some ways.

"The 'four great new inventions' have surely improved customer experience, and helped national and global economy __8__ at the same time," said Charlie Dai, principal analyst (首席分析师) of an American market research company.

As a whole, all the Chinese are __9__ of their four new inventions. It is increasingly clear that China is innovating and no longer copying western ideas. More and more foreigners __10__ to promote (促进) economic development in their countries by learning from China's innovation.

( ) 1. A. appeared   B. seemed   C. looked   D. showed
( ) 2. A. when   B. what   C. why   D. where
( ) 3. A. all   B. both   C. neither   D. none
( ) 4. A. in   B. on   C. to   D. from
( ) 5. A. improved   B. finished   C. invented   D. wasted
( ) 6. A. people   B. water   C. electricity D. money
( ) 7. A. to   B. in   C. on   D. by
( ) 8. A. develop   B. warn   C. mean   D. live
( ) 9. A. bored   B. tired   C. proud   D. satisfied
( ) 10. A. afford   B. repeat   C. hope   D. wait

三、阅读理解

阅读下面短文，从每题所给的 A、B、C、D 四个选项中选出最佳答案。

No technology is perfect: each innovation has advantages and disadvantages, as the following two examples show.

Many people predict that we'll be able to take to the skies in our own personal flying car. This technology would allow total freedom of movement. We could fly at 480 km per hour, avoiding traffic lights and busy roads. However, some believe there will be problems with traffic control. If the cars become popular, there is likely to be air traffic congestion（拥堵）. And what if the cars break down?

Also imagine having your own Iron Man（钢铁侠）suit. Several companies are trying to build a practical robot exoskeleton（外骨骼）. This is an electronic suit with robot arms and legs which follows the wearer's movements. It allows you to lift heavy objects, walk long distances and even punch（穿）through was! It will be of great help for armies, rescue workers and disabled people. The suit might help people walk again after disease or harm. However, one disadvantage at present is the cost. Even a simple exoskeleton can cost hundreds of thousands of pounds. Another problem is that a heavy suit like this needs a lot of power but battery life is short. These problems will no doubt be solved as lightweight plastic suits become available.

Looking ahead it's not difficult to imagine a future when we will be able to fly to work or lift a car above our heads. Although there are some problems to solve before all of these are possible, we can certainly dream of a world where technology makes life easier and safer for millions of people.

(　　)1. We can learn that flying cars might allow us to avoid _____.
   A. receiving speeding tickets
   B. traffic congestion in the air
   C. traffic congestion on the road
   D. losing traffic control on busy roads

(　　)2. The underlined word "It" in Paragraph 3 probably refers to the _____.
   A. robot exoskeleton   B. wearer's movement
   C. electronic Iron Man Suit   D. robot with arms and legs

(　　)3. The writer is sure that robot exoskeleton will become more _____.
   A. uncomfortable   B. expensive   C. available   D. impossible

(　　)4. Which of the following shows the medical use of robot suits?
   A. It allows the wearers to lift heavy things easily.

B. It might be able to help disabled people walk again.

C. It might help the wearers to walk long distances.

D. It makes it possible for the wearers to punch through walls.

(　　)5. The writer takes the flying car and the robot exoskeleton as examples to _____.

A. offer readers the latest information about development of new technology

B. show it's impossible to put these two kinds of technology to practical use

C. lead readers to buy the products of new technology as soon as possible

D. support his opinion that technology has advantages and disadvantages

四、书面表达

假如你的发明——为老人设计的智能手表(a smart watch)获得了成功,收到了很多人的好评,被推荐参加一个国际青少年科技展览。请你以"My Invention"为题用英语写一篇短文,介绍一下你的发明。

1. 提示词:easy to control; screen; show time; weather condition; location; make emergency calls; ￥499; be helpful to.

2. 要点包括:(1)智能手表的外观、功能和价格;(2)受到的好评。

3. 注意事项:(1)文中不得出现考生个人真实信息;(2)词数:80~100词;(3)开头和结尾已给出,不计入总词数。

My Invention

My invention is a smart watch for old people. It's simple and useful, and it's easy to control.

_____
_____
_____
_____
_____
_____

The watch is really helpful to old people.

Grammar

一、从下面每小题四个选项中选出最佳选项

( ) 1. The blue car is old, _____ my father still likes it very much.
  A. so   B. and   C. however   D. but

( ) 2. Follow the safety instructions, _____ you may get hurt.
  A. or   B. so   C. but   D. and

( ) 3. I feel very tired after a day's hard work, _____ I went to bed early.
  A. but   B. or   C. while   D. so

( ) 4. Bob _____ Bill don't study in the same school, _____ they are good friends.
  A. and; and   B. but; but   C. and; but   D. but; and

( ) 5. He speaks _____ English _____ French. Instead, he speaks Chinese.
  A. either; or   B. neither; nor
  C. not only; but also   D. not; but

( ) 6. Get up early tomorrow, _____ you'll catch the first bus.
  A. or   B. but   C. and   D. while

( ) 7. Either you or he _____ able to attend the meeting.
  A. is   B. am   C. are   D. be

( ) 8. There are many music lovers in his team. Some like singing, _____ others like listening.
  A. when   B. or   C. so   D. while

( ) 9. Sally likes apples _____ bananas, _____ she doesn't like pears.
  A. and; or   B. and; but   C. and; so   D. or; so

( ) 10. I called Jim last night, _____ he didn't answer the phone.
  A. either   B. neither   C. but   D. so

( ) 11. Give me a few minutes _____ I'll be able to finish it well.
  A. and   B. or   C. but   D. however

( ) 12. —Would you like to come to dinner this evening?
  —I'd like to, _____ I need to finish my homework first.
  A. if   B. but   C. or   D. and

Unit 7 Invention and Innovation

(   ) 13. Miss Ma didn't eat up all the food she ordered, _____ she took the rest away.
       A. when   B. while   C. or   D. so

(   ) 14. —I like to play football, _____ I don't have one.
       —I have a ball. Let's play together.
       A. but   B. and   C. so   D. or

(   ) 15. The meeting won't begin until 10:00, _____ there is no need for you to get up early.
       A. or   B. however   C. so   D. when

(   ) 16. Sweet snacks can give us energy, _____ they are not healthy for us.
       A. and   B. or   C. but   D. so

(   ) 17. Practice as hard as you can _____ you will win in the spoken English contest.
       A. or   B. and   C. for   D. but

(   ) 18. I am your friend _____ I will tell you the truth.
       A. so   B. or   C. either   D. while

(   ) 19. I like milk, _____, my mother doesn't like it at all.
       A. but   B. so   C. however   D. and

(   ) 20. Mr. Smith is 80 and he has just got a computer. _____ he doesn't know how to use it.
       A. But   B. Or   C. So   D. For

(   ) 21. Be careful, _____ you will make mistakes in the exam.
       A. and   B. but   C. so   D. or

(   ) 22. Mary liked the purse very much, _____ she couldn't afford it.
       A. and   B. or   C. but   D. so

(   ) 23. The shops were closed _____ I couldn't buy anything.
       A. for   B. so   C. although   D. or

(   ) 24. Mr. Yang was about to leave _____ his wife came back.
       A. when   B. while   C. until   D. but

(   ) 25. She tried to phone him, _____ there was no answer because he was abroad.
       A. since   B. while   C. but   D. however

(   ) 26. I study hard, _____ my little brother doesn't.
       A. but   B. and   C. so   D. or

(   ) 27. I must go back home before 10:30 pm _____ my father will be angry with me.
       A. and   B. or   C. so   D. but

(　　)28. I'm sorry to have to say this, _____ you forgot to turn off the light when left the room.

   A. however   B. or   C. but   D. and

(　　)29. We must hurry, _____ we will miss the early train.

   A. or   B. and   C. yet   D. so

(　　)30. Although square dancing is good exercise for the old, _____ sometimes it makes lots of noise.

   A. but   B. however   C. so   D. /

二、找出下列句子中错误的选项，并改正过来

1. The girl in red is new here, but few people know her.
   A B   C   D

2. Tom likes English, but he also likes math.
   A   B C D

3. Although many students were late yesterday, but Xiao Ming went to school on time.
  A   B   C   D

4. You'd better set out a little earlier, and you will be late for the meeting.
      A   B   C   D

5. I know the place well, but I think I can find it easily without a map.
      A B   C   D

6. The fridge is empty, so we had to go out for dinner tonight.
      A   B   C   D

7. Fred is from England, or he can speak Chinese very well.
   A   B C   D

8. I like dancing, for I don't have enough time to practice it.
    A   B C   D

9. The dress doesn't fit me well, so I don't want to buy them.
    A   B   D

10. Betty was silent at first, but soon she joins us, talking and laughing.
    A   B   C   D

1.(　　)应为_____ 2.(　　)应为_____ 3.(　　)应为_____

4.(　　)应为_____ 5.(　　)应为_____ 6.(　　)应为_____

7.(　　)应为_____ 8.(　　)应为_____ 9.(　　)应为_____

10.(　　)应为_____

Unit 7　Invention and Innovation

For Better Performance

一、找出与所给单词画线部分读音相同的选项

(　　) 1. sp<u>e</u>cial　　A. <u>e</u>xperience　　B. l<u>o</u>cal　　C. r<u>e</u>cord　　D. <u>a</u>ncient

(　　) 2. s<u>u</u>rround　　A. c<u>u</u>re　　B. man<u>u</u>al　　C. a<u>u</u>tumn　　D. s<u>u</u>ffer

(　　) 3. th<u>ea</u>ter　　A. id<u>ea</u>　　B. tr<u>ea</u>sure　　C. b<u>ea</u>ch　　D. f<u>ea</u>ture

(　　) 4. v<u>i</u>deo　　A. organ<u>i</u>ze　　B. <u>i</u>nform　　C. b<u>i</u>cycle　　D. pr<u>i</u>vate

(　　) 5. d<u>ou</u>btful　　A. s<u>ou</u>p　　B. c<u>ou</u>sin　　C. th<u>ou</u>sand　　D. t<u>ou</u>ch

二、英汉互译

1. invention _____

2. 经济 _____

3. distance _____

4. 政治 _____

5. development _____

6. 文化 _____

7. in the early 21th century _____

8. 梦想着 _____

9. at that time _____

10. 允许某人做某事 _____

三、用括号内所给汉语提示或单词的适当形式填空

1. There have been great _____ (发明) that change the way we live.

2. _____ (机器人) waiters are set to serve in the smart restaurant.

3. The elderly can give voice commands to _____ (operate) the robot for going out, dish washing and paying music.

4. We promote different models this season. Order one online and it is _____ (保证).

5. _____ (网络) of things refers to a network of real-world objects.

6. Because of the Internet, people are _____ (connect) with each other.

7. Technology allows us to do things we have never _____ (dream) of.

8. The wheel made it easier to carry heavy things and to travel long _____ (距离).

9. In the 19th century, the camera and light _____ (bulb) were invented.

10. Starting from the second half of the 20th century, man began looking for ways to go into _____ (太空).

四、找出下列句子中错误的选项,并改正过来

1. There has been great inventions that change the way we live.
      A   B   C   D

2. This invention made it easier to carry heavily things and to travel long distances.
                   A   B   C   D

3. The four great inventions of ancient China great promoted the development of our economy.
                  A   B   C   D

4. He failed many times, so he didn't give up.
      A   B   C   D

5. Many countries, included the United States and China, have made their steps into space, too.
                 A   B   C   D

1.(　) 应为_____　　2.(　) 应为_____　　3.(　) 应为_____
4.(　) 应为_____　　5.(　) 应为_____

单元检测

第一部分　英语知识运用(共分三节,满分40分)

第一节　语音知识:从A、B、C、D四个选项中找出其画线部分与所给单词画线部分读音相同的选项。(共5分,每小题1分)

(　)1. customer　　A. rubber　　B. unique　　C. bullet　　D. guest

(　)2. delivery　　A. section　　B. reception　　C. collect　　D. impress

(　)3. guarantee　　A. orange　　B. German　　C. larger　　D. garden

(　)4. innovation　　A. mother　　B. money　　C. second　　D. foreign

(　)5. introduce　　A. capability　　B. adequacy　　C. company　　D. atomic

第二节　词汇与语法知识:从A、B、C、D四个选项中选出可以填入空白处的最佳选项。(共25分,每小题1分)

(　)6. This type of drones can _____ coffee to people who are sleepy.
　　A. describe　　B. deliver　　C. buy　　D. sell

(　)7. At first, people were doubtful _____ the quality of the product bought online.
　　A. about　　B. with　　C. for　　D. in

(　)8. My electric car has _____ power.
　　A. run out　　B. eaten up　　C. run out of　　D. used up

Unit 7　Invention and Innovation

(　　) 9. Let me _____ the latest product to you.
　　A. buy　　　　B. prefer　　　　C. benefit　　　　D. introduce

(　　) 10. The 3D printer is still under _____.
　　A. guarantee　　B. video　　　　C. feature　　　　D. function

(　　) 11. The development of science and technology has _____ people's quality of life.
　　A. promote　　B. promotes　　　C. promoted　　　D. promoting

(　　) 12. We should attach great importance to technology, _____ we will fall behind.
　　A. and　　　　B. or　　　　　　C. so　　　　　　D. but

(　　) 13. The performance of the two products is _____.
　　A. similar　　　B. similarly　　　C. similarity　　　D. similarities

(　　) 14. All of us have benefited _____ the new technology and innovation.
　　A. of　　　　　B. about　　　　C. from　　　　　D. with

(　　) 15. Drones can _____ do many things in our daily life.
　　A. be used to　　B. be used for　　C. used to　　　　D. use to

(　　) 16. Everyone is surrounded by technology _____ a way.
　　A. by　　　　　B. on　　　　　　C. in　　　　　　D. to

(　　) 17. In the future people may live smart homes _____ you can turn lights on and off through your smart phone.
　　A. where　　　B. when　　　　C. which　　　　D. why

(　　) 18. We don't allow _____ at school.
　　A. smoke　　　B. to smoke　　　C. smoked　　　　D. smoking

(　　) 19. _____ Tom, his parents also went to the film last weekend.
　　A. Beside　　　B. Besides　　　　C. But　　　　　D. Except

(　　) 20. —What is the _____ of this product?
　　—It can break down food.
　　A. size　　　　B. colour　　　　C. price　　　　　D. function

(　　) 21. Frank enjoyed his new school life _____ making new friends.
　　A. by　　　　　B. to　　　　　　C. for　　　　　　D. from

(　　) 22. —What do you think _____ it?
　　—It's good in quality and cheap in price.
　　A. of　　　　　B. with　　　　　C. for　　　　　　D. from

(　　) 23. Keep working hard, and you will surely succeed _____.
　　A. earlier and later　　　　　　B. sooner and later
　　C. earlier or later　　　　　　　D. sooner or later

( )24. They prefer _____ at home to shopping at weekends.

    A. to read   B. read   C. reading   D. reads

( )25. _____, he is just a child. He made such a terrible mistake.

    A. After all   B. First of all   C. Not at all   D. All right

( ) 26. Nowadays people can order their food online and get it _____ to their doorsteps.

    A. deliver   B. to deliver   C. delivering   D. delivered

( )27. Don't forget to _____ your computer when you leave the office.

    A. turn on   B. turn off   C. turn up   D. turn down

( ) 28. In order to make lives _____ and more comfortable, they have to work longer hours.

    A. easily   B. easier   C. more easily   D. easiest

( )29. During the job interview, you will talk with the manager face _____ face.

    A. by   B. in   C. to   D. on

( )30. A lot of new technologies have been _____ to our home.

    A. introduced   B. introduce

    C. introduces   D. introducing

第三节 完形填空：阅读下面的短文，从所给的 A、B、C、D 四个选项中选出正确的答案。(共 10 分，每小题 1 分)

Nature is full of great ideas. Many inventors watch nature for ideas to make some __31__ things For example, a new type of cane(手杖) was invented to help blind people move around more __32__. And the idea behind this invention came from the bat.

How Bats Get Around

Bats make sounds when they fly at night. These sounds can't be heard by people __33__ they help bats fly in the dark.

Bats send out sound waves through their mouth or nose when they fly. If these sound waves __34__ objects around them, they will be sent back as an echo(回声). The echo tells bats how far away things __35__ trees are. It also helps them know __36__ to find something to eat.

A Batty Idea

After watching how bats fly, the scientist who invented the new cane first built a lightweight cane, and then to it he __37__ device(装置) that sends and receives the same sound waves as bats do while flying. Finally, he __38__ the cane. It worked out!

How the Cane Works

The cane sends out sound waves. When an echo is sent back, the top of the cane vibrates

(震动). This helps the person 39 the cane know how far away an object is. They will also know how big the object is.

The 40 of the cane shows that nature is really where great ideas come from.

( )31. A. useful   B. interesting   C. polite   D. private
( )32. A. quickly   B. smoothly   C. slowly   D. wisely
( )33. A. so   B. because   C. although   D. but
( )34. A. see   B. hit   C. explore   D. research
( )35. A. like   B. as   C. under   D. above
( )36. A. why   B. when   C. where   D. what
( )37. A. added   B. designed   C. improved   D. increased
( )38. A. used   B. bought   C. tested   D. sold
( )39. A. trying   B. making   C. following   D. holding
( )40. A. instruction B. invention   C. information D. introduction

第二部分　篇章与词汇理解(共分三节,满分 50 分)

第一节　阅读理解:阅读下列短文,从每题所给的 A、B、C、D 四个选项中,选出最恰当的答案。(共 30 分,每小题 2 分)

A

When you are hungry, drawing a picture of a hamburger will not make you feel full. However, thanks to a new product from a Japanese printing company, you can eat the paper that you draw on.

Moeka Hoda and Kanako Murakami work for this company. Not long after the two had joined the company, they took part in a project. They were asked to find a problem that people always meet with and then try to solve it.

Hoda and Murakami used the Internet for ideas. One complaint caught their eyes "We can't eat anything during class," wrote one student. "When I get hungry, my stomach makes a big noise." To help people with the same problem, Hoda and Murakami made a special set of notepads and pens. They used paper made from potato starch, oil and water. The pen's ink was made from water, citric acid and coloring.

The two young men posted a video of their product on the Internet. To their surprise, many people liked it. Soon, the company started selling these notepads and pens. During three weeks, more than 500 sets were sold. Lots of customers are probably already eating their notes.

( )41. The new product can help _____ people.

　　　A. hungry　　　B. thirsty　　　C. full　　　D. sad

( )42. The underlined word "complaint" in Paragraph 3 means _____ in Chinese.

　　　A. 鼓励　　　B. 满意　　　C. 抱怨　　　D. 失望

( )43. Where did Hoda and Murakami get the idea?

　　　A. From the company.　　　B. On the Internet.

　　　C. In the supermarket.　　　D. From a pen factory.

( )44. What may happen when many people use the product according to the passage?

　　　A. Students can eat a real hamburger during class.

　　　B. Cooks will lose their jobs.

　　　C. Mothers will not need to cook.

　　　D. The drawing paper is not bad to eat.

( )45. What can we learn from the passage?

　　　A. The product was not popular.

　　　B. The special notepads sold well.

　　　C. The pen's link was made from soup.

　　　D. People don't eat the special notepads.

B

For a long time, the rest of the world only knew China's four major inventions: the compass, gunpowder, paper-making and printing. However, China has once again changed the world with its "new four great inventions": high-speed railways, electronic payments, shared bicycles and online shopping.

The new four great inventions are related to China's high-tech innovation, which improves the quality of people's lives.

"My wallet is no longer in use. I can buy and eat whatever I want simply with my phone," said Lin Jinlong, an overseas Chinese student from Cambodia, adding that even pancake sellers are using Alipay (mobile payment). "We can also order food at home, which is super convenient. If I were at home in Cambodia, I would have to go outdoors."

As a huge fan of bicycles, Lin also expressed his love for China's shared bicycles, saying that "shared bikes are bringing cycling back to people's lives. They are making public transport more convenient and encouraging people to be more active."

Lin said that travelling by Chinese high-speed train from Beijing to Tianjin, which is more than 1,000 km away, takes only half an hour, while in Cambodia, such a journey may take up to three hours.

It is clear that China is innovating and no longer copying western ideas. This is especially true in mobile, where China is leading in many ways such as social messaging app WeChat. China has the largest mobile use in the world.

( )46. _____ is Not one of the new four great inventions.
  A. Paper-making   B. Shared bicycles
  C. High-speed railways   D. Electronic payment

( )47. What does the underlined word "electronic" in Paragraph 1 mean?
  A. 自动的 B. 风力的 C. 电子的 D. 发电的

( )48. Which of the following is True according to the passage?
  A. The world only know China's four major inventions now.
  B. People in Cambodia can buy everything with their phones.
  C. Alipay is a kind of electronic payment that is only used by pancake sellers.
  D. The new four great inventions have relation to China's high technology.

( )49. We can learn that _____ from the passage.
  A. shared bikes are not convenient
  B. shared bikes are faster than high-speed trains
  C. mobile phones are widely used in China
  D. it takes 3 hours from Beijing to Tianjin by high-speed train

( )50. The passage mainly talks about _____.
  A. China's four major inventions
  B. China's new four great inventions
  C. the experience of a student from Cambodia
  D. China's high-tech innovation

C

People often use their phones to take pictures of their meals especially delicious ones to share online. But Clear Plate, a WeChat min-program, encourages you to take pictures of your empty plates after a meal. The program's AI "see" that your plates are empty and gives you points. You can use these points to buy yourself gifts or give away the points to buy meals for children in poor areas.

The program was developed by Liu, a student at Tsinghua University. Liu came up with the idea in 2017. "Technological innovation is a good way to cut down food waste," said Liu. He put together a 20-member team to work on the program. To teach the program's AI how to recognize empty plates, the team spent half a year collecting 100,000 photo samples from cafes and restaurants in 10 cities.

The team also started a campaign called Clear Your Plate in Chinese universities in 2018. Students competed against each other to see who could get those most points in Clear Plate. In its third year, the one-month campaign reached 1,017 schools. In 2020, almost 1.6 million people took part in it, cutting down food waste by 862 tons.

Thanks to his work, Liu was named by the United Nations in the list of 2020 Class of Young Leaders for Sustainable(可持续发展的)Development Goals. "We hope our efforts can encourage young people to value their food and develop the habit of thrift(节俭)," Liu said.

(　　)51. How did Clear Plate encourage people to take pictures of empty plates after a meal?

　　A. It gives points that people can use to buy things.

　　B. It gives away meals to people for free.

　　C. It sends gifts to people with high scores.

　　D. It makes people compete against each other.

(　　)52. Liu's team developed the program in order to _____.

　　A. collect photo samples of food

　　B. cur down food waste

　　C. teach people to take beautiful pictures

　　D. help children in poor areas

(　　)53. What can we learn about the campaign Clear Your Plate?

　　A. It was first started in middle schools.

　　B. It lasts for a whole year.

　　C. It brings lots of good.

　　D. It attracts a small number of students.

(　　)54. What do you think of Liu?

　　A. Lazy.　　　B. Foolish.　　　C. Selfish.　　　D. Creative.

(　　)55. What's the best title for the passage?

　　A. A Funny Wechat Mini-Program.

　　B. A New Fashion of Taking Pictures.

　　C. Liu—A Great Hero.

　　D. Clearing Your Plate With Technology.

第二节　词义搭配：从(B)栏中选出(A)栏单词的正确解释。(共**10**分，每小题**1**分)

　　　　(A)　　　　　　　　　　　(B)

(　　)56. benefit　　　A. the act of delivering or distributing something

(　　)57. besides　　　B. what something is used for

( )58. customer   C. be beneficial for

( )59. delivery   D. cause to come to know personally

( )60. feature   E. any unwanted and destructive insect or other animal

( )61. function   F. someone who pays for goods or services

( )62. innovation   G. in addition

( )63. introduce   H. a prominent attribute or aspect of something

( )64. operate   I. the creation of something in the mind

( )65. pest   J. direct or control

第三节 补全对话：根据对话内容，从对话后的选项中选出能填入空白处的最佳选项。(共 10 分，每小题 2 分)

A：Look at this picture. __66__

B：Oh, it's a robot.

A：You're right. It's the newest robot in the world.

B：__67__

A：It can help with housework.

B：Can it sweep the floor?

A：Of course. It can sweep the floor. It can also take care of kids and old people.

B：__68__

A：No, I won't. Because it's too expensive for me.

B：__69__

A：15,000 dollars. We can have a look at it tomorrow. It is on show in the Science Museum.

B：Sounds great. Let's go and see it together. When shall we meet?

A：__70__ OK?

B：OK. See you then.

A. What can it do?
B. Let's meet at 9:00 am.
C. Will you buy it?
D. What's it?
E. How much is it?

第三部分 语言技能应用(共分四节,满分30分)

第一节 单词拼写:根据下列句子及所给汉语注释,在相应题号后的横线上写出该单词的正确形式。(共5分,每小题1分)

71. The new hospital will _____(有益于) the entire community.

72. My father asked me to see the _____(顾客) to the door.

73. Please send this parcel by express _____(递送).

74. Wet weather is a _____(特征) of life in this area.

75. The teacher didn't explain its grammatical _____(功能).

第二节 词形变换:用括号内单词的适当形式填空。(共5分,每小题1分)

76. I _____ (guarantee) that this will not happen again.

77. Excuse me, may I take the opportunity to _____(introduction) myself?

78. It's too difficult for him to _____ (operation) the new machine.

79. Stores of grain are often attacked by _____ (pest).

80. I would _____ (prefer) to stay at home rather than go out on such a rainy day.

第三节 改错:从 A、B、C、D 四个画线处找出一处错误的选项,填入括号内,并在横线上写出正确答案。(共10分,每小题2分)

81. The refrigerator <u>can</u> be <u>managing</u> by <u>giving</u> voice <u>commands</u>.
       A B   C   D

82. <u>It</u> is <u>easily</u> to <u>operate</u>, <u>especially</u> for elderly people.
 A B   C   D

83. A <u>guest</u> is <u>interesting</u> <u>in</u> the <u>use</u> of drones.
  A   B   C   D

84. I <u>want to pick</u> a drone <u>what</u> can help me <u>on the farm</u>.
  A B   C   D

85. I <u>want</u> the type <u>with</u> <u>highly</u> quality and <u>reasonable</u> price.
  A   B C   D

81.( ) 应为_____ 82.( ) 应为_____ 83.( ) 应为_____

84.( ) 应为_____ 85.( ) 应为_____

第四节 书面表达。(共10分)

假如你是李芳,你校上月举行了青少年科技创新大赛,鼓励发明创造。你的发明作品"飞翔单车(flying bike)"荣获了一等奖。你的英国笔友玛丽对你的发明很感兴趣,请你给玛丽写一封邮件介绍你的发明。

1. 提示词:wings, solar power, wind power, wake up, faster than, pollute air.

2. 写作要点:(1)飞翔单车的外观与特点;(2)飞翔单车的优点。

3. 注意事项：(1)文中不得出现考生个人真实信息；(2)词数:80~100 词；
(3)开头和结尾已给出，不计入总词数。

Dear Mary,

  I am writing to introduce my invention to you. _____
_____
_____
_____
_____
_____
_____

Yours,
Li Fang

Unit 8

Green Earth

Warming-up

一、句型汇总

1. What is the picture about? 这幅图是关于什么的?
2. What is the animal in the picture? 图中是什么动物?
3. Where does it take place? 它发生在哪里?
4. It takes place in Arctic. 它发生在北极。

二、英汉互译

1. melt _____
2. 塑料_____
3. pollution _____
4. 雾霾_____
5. Arctic _____
6. 北极熊_____
7. ice _____
8. 破坏_____
9. cloth bag _____
10. 全球变暖_____
11. garbage sorting _____
12. 发生_____

Unit 8　Green Earth

Listening and Speaking

一、找出与所给单词画线部分读音相同的选项

(　　) 1. dis<u>a</u>ppear　　A. ch<u>a</u>racter　　B. str<u>a</u>ight　　C. pl<u>a</u>nt　　D. <u>a</u>dvice

(　　) 2. b<u>o</u>ttle　　A. dr<u>o</u>p　　B. c<u>o</u>lour　　C. cust<u>o</u>mer　　D. intr<u>o</u>duce

(　　) 3. d<u>u</u>stbin　　A. <u>u</u>seful　　B. b<u>u</u>s　　C. abo<u>u</u>t　　D. red<u>u</u>ce

(　　) 4. Arct<u>i</u>c　　A. c<u>e</u>ll　　B. r<u>e</u>cycle　　C. <u>i</u>ce　　D. <u>e</u>ffect

(　　) 5. <u>e</u>ffect　　A. prot<u>e</u>ct　　B. m<u>e</u>lt　　C. <u>e</u>lectricity　　D. b<u>e</u>nefit

二、从(B)栏中找出与(A)栏中相对应的答语

(A)

1. What does it say?
2. What are the new dustbins for?
3. I don't know how to do that.
4. Is it because of the global warming?
5. Why should we do this?

(B)

A. You are right.
B. In order to protect our earth.
C. It says the Arctic ice cover is becoming smaller and smaller every year.
D. Don't worry. Here is a handbook about it.
E. For garbage sorting.

三、用所给句子补全下面对话

A：Hi, Jason. ___1___

B：Hi, Peter. I went to Guangzhou to take part in a meeting about protection. And I met a student from a green school there.

A：A green school? ___2___

B：It's a school which supports the protection of the environment.

A：___3___

B：They collect waste things and save energy, such as electricity and water.

A：Wow! If everyone tries to protect the environment like them, the earth will become better.

B：___4___

A：Are there any green schools in other places of China?

B: Yes. ___5___

A: I think we should also do something to protect our environment.

B: So do I.

> A. In fact, there are thousands of green schools in other places of China.
> B. I agree with you.
> C. What's that?
> D. Where did you go yesterday afternoon?
> E. What do the teachers and students do in a green school?

四、场景模拟

编写一组对话,和你的朋友谈论保护环境的措施。

提示词汇:hot; drive cars; cut down trees; global warming; make a poster; protect the earth.

Reading and Writing

一、用括号内所给汉语提示或单词的适当形式填空

1. Everyone should put rubbish into _____ (dustbin).

2. All these _____ (bottle) are made of glass.

3. The number of some wild animals is _____ (下降).

4. Polar _____ (bear) have to find food under the sea.

5. If you don't know how to do that, you can look at this _____ (手册).

6. After being _____ (recycle), the waste can be made into other materials.

7. The Arctic ice cover is becoming smaller and smaller because of the _____ (globe)

warming.

8. We should do what we can to _____ (保护) our environment.

9. Can you give me some examples about kitchen _____ (garbage)?

10. After special treatment, they can be used to _____ (generate) power.

二、完形填空

"Green" is more than just a color. It means that you should live to __1__ the environment—the water, the land and the air. You can be a green kid by following these steps.

Reduce it. When you __2__ less of something, you do a good thing for the earth. For example, a __3__ shower means you use less water. Turn off the water when you are __4__ your teeth.

Reuse it. Many times, even if you don't need one thing, someone else might just need it. __5__ example, if you don't want to play with the toy bear, you can give it to your neighbour. Try to __6__ books, toys, even clothes with friends.

Enjoy it. It's true that __7__ is a great problem now, but the earth is still a beautiful and interesting place to explore (探索). Go for a hike, visit nature centers and gardens, climb mountains and take a __8__ in the rivers…Outdoor __9__ are good for you. You can also plant trees, collect reusable things… __10__ a green kid is so easy.

( ) 1. A. protect   B. print   C. paint   D. permit
( ) 2. A. usable   B. useless   C. useful   D. use
( ) 3. A. longer   B. shorter   C. more   D. bigger
( ) 4. A. brush   C. brushes   C. brushing   D. brushed
( ) 5. A. As   B. For   C. By   D. With
( ) 6. A. change   B. buy   C. sell   D. borrow
( ) 7. A. pollute   B. polluted   C. pollution   D. polluting
( ) 8. A. plane   B. boat   C. taxi   D. subway
( ) 9. A. activities   B. activity   C. active   D. act
( ) 10. A. Become   B. Becomes   C. Became   D. Becoming

三、阅读理解

阅读下面短文,从每题所给的 A、B、C、D 四个选项中选出最佳答案。

One day, Paula Ma was walking along Castle Island's beach. She found there were lots of plastic pieces in the sea and some were too small to pick up. She began to think about how to solve the problem.

First, she did a survey. The result showed there were already 150 million tons of plastic in the sea and every year there would be another 8 million tons. She realized something must be done. So she decided to invent a robot that could work under water. She tried again and again. At last her ROV came out. It could move through water and pick up plastic pieces, especially the small ones.

With this ROV, Paula Ma took part in the Broadcom Masters competition. It was one of the top STEM competitions. It's for young students around the world. This year, more than 5,000 students were interested in the competition, but only a few got the chance. Paula Ma's ROV caught a lot of attention. It has a camera with three different kinds of lights. It could find plastic pieces easily. Dana Yoerger, an expert, said, "The ROV is nicely done for a 12-year-old girl. It's very clever."

In fact, Paula Ma is always learning to solve the world problems and her parents are always supporting her. At the age of five, she began to go to workshops to learn engineering skills. When she was asked about the future plan, she said, "I want to be an engineer because I like building things. I think many world problems can be solved with new inventions. Right now, I'm just caring about plastic problems because there is still a long way to go."

( ) 1. Paula Ma found that _____ in her survey.

　　A. some robots work under water at that time

　　B. 150 million tons of plastic was found on Castle Island

　　C. there would be more and more plastic pieces in the sea

　　D. many people were picking up plastic pieces on the beach

( ) 2. _____, Paula Ma invented her ROV.

　　A. To help her move through deep water

　　B. To pick up basketballs in the sea

　　C. To cut plastic in the sea into pieces

　　D. To pick up plastic pieces in the sea

( ) 3. We can learn from Dana Yoerger's words that _____.

　　A. she thinks highly of the ROV

　　B. ROV is made for young girls

　　C. the competition is well organized

　　D. some young girls are very clever

( ) 4. Paula Ma wanted to be an engineer because she wanted to _____.

　　A. keep the sea clean　　　　　　B. invent things to solve problems

　　C. learn engineer skills　　　　　　D. realize her parents' future plan

( ) 5. Which is the correct order of the following events?

　　① Paula Ma invented her ROV.

Unit 8 Green Earth

② Paula Ma took part in the Broadcom Masters competition.

③ Paula Ma walked along Castle Island's beach.

④ Paula Ma began to learn engineer skills in workplace.

A. ③②①④ B. ②③④① C. ②①③④ D. ④③①②

四、书面表达

假如你是某职业学校的学生张磊,在网上看到中国环境保护协会(China Environmental Protection Association,CEPA)正面向全国招募500名志愿者,以便开展环境保护知识的普及活动。你想申请成为其中一员,请用英语写一封自荐信。

1. 提示词:online;volunteer;one of the members;air pollution;water pollution;play a part in;be good at;knowledge;protect.

2. 要点包括:(1)说明写信目的;(2)简述个人情况和优势;(3)表达期望。

3. 注意事项:(1)文中不得出现考生个人真实信息;(2)词数:80~100词;(3)开头和结尾已给出,不计入总词数。

Dear Sir/Madam,

　　I'm Zhang Lei, a vocational school student.

_____
_____
_____
_____
_____
_____

Yours sincerely,
Zhang Lei

Grammar

一、从下面每小题四个选项中选出最佳选项

(　　)1. It is he _____ up with the new idea, so we think he is creative.

A. who comes　　B. who come　　C. whom comes　　D. whom come

(   )2. It was our teacher _____ helped us solve the problem finally.
   A. whom   B. which   C. that   D. whose

(   )3. It is you _____ against the plan, because it sounds impossible to carry out.
   A. that is   B. who are   C. who am   D. that was

(   )4. It is once a month _____ John visited his parents after he got a job in the new company.
   A. when   B. where   C. who   D. that

(   )5. Don't take animal signs or star signs so seriously. _____ you who shape your life.
   A. This is   B. That is   C. It is   D. They are

(   )6. It's what you're doing now _____ will make a difference to your future.
   A. that   B. what   C. which   D. who

(   )7. It is not who is right but what is right _____ is of importance.
   A. which   B. it   C. this   D. that

(   )8. It is at 11 pm yesterday night _____ he came back from work.
   A. when   B. that   C. what   D. which

(   )9. _____ was _____ who I met in the library this morning.
   A. It; whom   B. It; he   C. That; he   D. That; him

(   )10. It was not until midnight _____ the noise of the street stopped.
   A. that   B. which   C. since   D. when

(   )11. It was not until he came back last night _____ he told me what had happened.
   A. when   B. which   C. that   D. whom

(   )12. It was in 2,000 _____ I graduated from university.
   A. when   B. who   C. where   D. that

(   )13. It is I who _____ going to Beijing on business next week.
   A. am   B. is   C. are   D. was

(   )14. It was _____ that I went shopping yesterday.
   A. my mother   B. with my mother   C. my sister   D. my friend

(   )15. It is the ability to do the job _____ matters not where you're from or what you are.
   A. who   B. whom   C. whose   D. that

(   )16. It was at the very beginning _____ Mr. Black made a decision that we should send for a doctor.
   A. that   B. when   C. who   D. what

(   ) 17. It was _____ who helped us out of danger.
　　　　A. them　　　B. they　　　C. their　　　D. theirs

(   ) 18. It was because I was your friend _____ I spoke out frankly.
　　　　A. why　　　B. because　　　C. how　　　D. that

(   ) 19. It was because I was caught in the heavy rain _____ I came to school late yesterday.
　　　　A. which　　　B. why　　　C. that　　　D. how

(   ) 20. It was my sister _____ met Mary in the street last night.
　　　　A. whose　　　B. who　　　C. whom　　　D. she

(   ) 21. It is Tom _____ the window just now in the classroom.
　　　　A. who broke　　　B. who breaks　　　C. whom broke　　　D. whom breaks

(   ) 22. It is at the foot of the hill _____ we plant trees every year.
　　　　A. where　　　B. in which　　　C. that　　　D. who

(   ) 23. It was because of bad weather _____ our football match had to be put off.
　　　　A. why　　　B. so　　　C. therefore　　　D. that

(   ) 24. It was _____ his wife came back _____ he turned off the light.
　　　　A. not until; that
　　　　B. not until; when
　　　　C. until; that
　　　　D. until; when

(   ) 25. It is _____ that Mike often drink in the afternoon.
　　　　A. bread　　　B. hamburgers　　　C. dumplings　　　D. coffee

(   ) 26. _____ five books that she lent me last month.
　　　　A. It was　　　B. It were　　　C. That was　　　D. That were

(   ) 27. It was on the phone _____ I talked to my teacher for an hour.
　　　　A. how　　　B. that　　　C. where　　　D. when

(   ) 28. It is on weekends _____ my brother often plays basketball in the gym.
　　　　A. when　　　B. where　　　C. who　　　D. that

(   ) 29. It is not _____ midnight that his father came back from the company.
　　　　A. when　　　B. until　　　C. while　　　D. till

(   ) 30. It is Mr. Yang _____ us English.
　　　　A. who teaches
　　　　B. who teach
　　　　C. whom teaches
　　　　D. whom teach

二、找出下列句子中错误的选项，并改正过来

1. It is my mother who are going shopping tomorrow.
   　A　B　　　　　C　D

2. It was in the park where I met my good friend this morning.
   　A　B　　　　　　C　D

3. That was my teacher who helped me improve my spoken English.
   　A　　　　　　　　B　　C　　　D

4. It is he that I often ask for help when I'm in trouble.
   　A　B　C　　　　　　　　D

5. It was because he was ill why he didn't go to school last Friday.
   　A　　B　　　　　　　C　　D

6. It is my sister who often help me clean my room.
   　A　　　　　　B　　　C　　D

7. It was October 1st that New China was founded.
   　A　　B　　　　C　　　　　D

8. It was by Xiao Li's help that I found my lost cat.
   　A　　B　　　　　　　C　　D

9. It was yesterday that my friend meets Li Ming.
   　A　B　　　　　C　　　　　D

10. It was I who see the accident in the street yesterday evening.
    　　A　B　C　　　　　　　　　　　　　D

1.（　）应为_____　2.（　）应为_____　3.（　）应为_____
4.（　）应为_____　5.（　）应为_____　6.（　）应为_____
7.（　）应为_____　8.（　）应为_____　9.（　）应为_____
10.（　）应为_____

For Better Performance

一、找出与所给单词画线部分读音相同的选项

（　）1. gl<u>o</u>bal　　A. l<u>o</u>ck　　　B. c<u>o</u>ver　　C. ph<u>o</u>to　　D. kingd<u>o</u>m

（　）2. tr<u>ea</u>tment　A. b<u>ea</u>r　　　B. str<u>ea</u>m　　C. d<u>ea</u>d　　D. h<u>ea</u>d

（　）3. w<u>a</u>ste　　　A. <u>a</u>ffect　　B. dist<u>a</u>nce　C. spr<u>a</u>y　　D. w<u>a</u>rn

（　）4. handb<u>oo</u>k　A. bamb<u>oo</u>　B. p<u>oo</u>l　　　C. t<u>oo</u>　　　D. childh<u>oo</u>d

（　）5. r<u>ea</u>lize　　A. app<u>ea</u>r　　B. b<u>ea</u>r　　　C. f<u>ea</u>ture　D. tr<u>ea</u>sure

二、英汉互译

1. realize _____ 2. 保护 _____

3. call on _____ 4. 关闭 _____

5. in this way _____ 6. 注意 _____

7. around the world _____ 8. 高达 _____

9. such as _____ 10. 参加 _____

三、用括号内所给汉语提示或单词的适当形式填空

1. Work hard and you will _____ (实现) your dream.

2. Please _____ (turn) off the light when you leave the room.

3. People should pay more _____ (注意, 留心) to climate change.

4. One fourth of the students in our class took _____ (part) in the sports meeting.

5. We're trying to do something _____ (专门的) to protect our earth.

6. Make a _____ (调查) on the things you and your classmates don't go green about.

7. Find out the top three and _____ (讨论) the possible solutions.

8. If you're ready to go green, start by _____ (change) your mind and personal habits.

9. Earth hour is a _____ (全球的) event held on the last Saturday of March every year.

10. Not everyone has realized the _____ (重要性) of recycling.

四、找出下列句子中错误的选项, 并改正过来

1. It means to take special steps to protect the environment.
    A   B   C   D

2. It is people's choices what cause pollution in our world.
   A   B   C   D

3. Here is a four-steps guide to being green.
   A   B   C D

4. That is in the park that he met his friend.
   A   B   C D

5. In order to be green, we can reducing the resources we use.
   A   B   C   D

1.( ) 应为 _____ 2.( ) 应为 _____ 3.( ) 应为 _____

4.( ) 应为 _____ 5.( ) 应为 _____

单元检测

第一部分 英语知识运用(共分三节,满分40分)

第一节 语音知识：从 A、B、C、D 四个选项中找出其画线部分与所给单词画线部分读音相同的选项。(共5分,每小题1分)

( )1. childhood   A. distance   B. disappear   C. dustbin   D. realize

( )2. pollution   A. function   B. structure   C. include   D. unique

( )3. restore   A. result   B. special   C. physical   D. reserve

( )4. neighbor   A. weight   B. receive   C. foreign   D. neither

( )5. transportation   A. world   B. work   C. fork   D. sailor

第二节 词汇与语法知识：从 A、B、C、D 四个选项中选出可以填入空白处的最佳选项。(共25分,每小题1分)

( )6. Take care! The waste might be _____.
     A. healthy   B. toxic   C. danger   D. slight

( )7. We will clear all the _____ at the seaside this Sunday.
     A. bottle   B. plant   C. battery   D. pollution

( )8. Everyone can always go green by _____ while moving around.
     A. driving cars   B. taking public transportation
     C. take shared bicycles   D. throwing waste

( )9. It was not until we told him the truth _____ he realized he made a mistake.
     A. that   B. when   C. how   D. why

( )10. I don't want to get _____ in everyone's business.
     A. involving   B. involved   C. contain   D. include

( )11. It was a new bike that he _____ last weekend.
     A. buy   B. buys   C. bought   D. buying

( )12. _____ people's choice that causes pollution in the world.
     A. That be   B. That is   C. It be   D. It is

( )13. It was after learning this dialogue _____ I knew the importance of recycling.
     A. which   B. that   C. who   D. what

( )14. It's time _____ us to take actions for our next generations.
     A. of   B. about   C. for   D. with

( ) 15. Billions of plastic bags _____ each year around the world.
   A. is used   B. are used   C. is using   D. are using

( ) 16. At this restaurant, dessert is _____ in the price of the meal.
   A. include   B. includes   C. included   D. including

( ) 17. Trees also offer several benefits _____ human beings.
   A. to   B. for   C. with   D. /

( ) 18. Living in China has been a wonderful _____ for Mr. White.
   A. experienced   B. experiencing   C. experiences   D. experience

( ) 19. Kitchen garbage can _____ feeding animals or made into plant food.
   A. be used to   B. be used for   C. used to   D. use to

( ) 20. —Can you recycle these _____ metal cans?
   —Yes, we can use them to make works of art.
   A. use   B. uses   C. using   D. used

( ) 21. There were different _____ fish in the stream.
   A. kinds of   B. kind of   C. kinds   D. kind

( ) 22. I used to have _____ in the beautiful environment.
   A. a lot of funs B. a lot of fun   C. a lot funs   D. a lot fun

( ) 23. In recent years, some changes _____ in my hometown.
   A. has happened   B. have happened
   C. has taken place   D. have taken place

( ) 24. Don't leave the tap _____ while washing your hands.
   A. run   B. runs   C. running   D. ran

( ) 25. If we all _____ it, we will be able to make our world more beautiful.
   A. take part in B. took part in   C. join   D. joined

( ) 26. Harmful waste can be made into other materials after _____ treatment.
   A. especially   B. specially   C. specialty   D. special

( ) 27. Arctic sea ice is melting _____ global warming.
   A. because   B. because of   C. since   D. as

( ) 28. John Smith is _____ a community clerk about garbage sorting.
   A. talk about   B. talking about
   C. talk with   D. talking with

( ) 29. We can put used batteries to good use _____ throwing them away.
   A. fond of   B. instead of   C. proud of   D. demand of

(   )30. We shouldn't _____ here when we see the following sign.

A. throw rubbish   B. eat anything

C. speak loudly   D. make noise

第三节　完形填空：阅读下面的短文，从所给的 A、B、C、D 四个选项中选出正确的答案。(共 10 分，每小题 1 分)

Hello, human friends. My name is Nick. I am __31__ turtle. I have __32__ in the ocean for over half a century.

In general, turtles can live to be __33__ than 100 years old. But now many of my fellow(同伴) turtles are dying because of one thing: plastic.

Human beings use too much plastic. When you throw plastic __34__, it doesn't just disappear. Over 90% percent of the world's plastic doesn't get recycled. A lot of plastic ends up in the __35__.

Most of my fellows do not know the __36__ of plastic. They think it is food. But in fact, plastic is poisonous. Around 30 percent of my fellows have plastic in their stomach. I have plastic in my body, __37__.

The plastic is also killing other sea animals. Last month, one of my whale friends died after eating 80 plastic bags. I feel so __38__ about it.

My human friends, please stop __39__ so much plastic. Maybe one plastic bag or one coffee cup won't make a difference, but when seven billion people all start to use __40__ plastic, we are living a better life.

(   )31. A. the   B. a   C. an   D. /
(   )32. A. live   B. lives   C. lived   D. living
(   )33. A. more   B. many   C. much   D. most
(   )34. A. into   B. in   C. away   D. on
(   )35. A. land   B. air   C. forest   D. ocean
(   )36. A. danger   B. endanger   C. dangerous   D. dangerously
(   )37. A. either   B. too   C. also   D. neither
(   )38. A. happy   B. excited   C. sad   D. pleased
(   )39. A. to use   B. use   C. used   D. using
(   )40. A. less   B. fewer   C. little   D. few

第二部分　篇章与词汇理解(共分三节,满分50分)

第一节　阅读理解：阅读下列短文,从每题所给的 **A、B、C、D** 四个选项中,选出最恰当的答案。(共30分,每小题2分)

A

The following is a quiz(测验)from a magazine：			
Questions	1 Point	2 Points	3 Points
Where do you live?	In a village.	In a town.	In a city.
How do you go to work/school?	Walking/By bike.	By train/bus/subway.	Driving a car.
How many times a year do you fly on planes?	0–2	3–5	More than 5.
How many hours of electricity do you use each day?	0–6 hours.	6–12 hours.	12–18 hours.
How often do you recycle?	Always.	Often.	Sometimes.
Total points	Result		
5–7	Less pollution than the average person(普通人).		
8–10	As much pollution as the average person.		
11–13	A little more pollution than the average person.		
14–15	A lot more pollution than the average person.		

(　　)41. The passage is probably from a/an _____.

　　A. newspaper　　　　　　　　B. advertisement

　　C. magazine　　　　　　　　D. story book

(　　)42. Which of the following makes the least pollution?

　　A. Always recycling used things.

　　B. Flying on planes three times a year.

　　C. Living pretty well in a big city.

　　D. Using 15 hours of electricity each day.

(　　)43. How many points does the average person get?

　　A. 5–7 hours.　　　　　　　　B. 8–10 points.

　　C. 11–13 points.　　　　　　D. 14–15 points.

(　　)44. Mike lives in a big city, goes to school by subway, flies on planes once a year, uses 15 hours of electricity a day, and sometimes recycles used things. How many points does he get?

　　A. 11 points.　　B. 12 points.　　C. 13 points.　　D. 14 points.

(　　)45. Which is the best title for the quiz?

　　A. Where Do You Live?　　B. Why Do You Recycle?
　　C. Why Do We Travel?　　D. How Green Are You?

B

Do you know anyone who plays Ant Forest? It is a game on Alipay. Users collect energy for their tree to grow. When their tree finishes growing, Alipay will plant a real tree in the desert areas of China.

This is part of China's efforts to fight <u>desertification</u>. China has planted more than 66 billion trees across its dry northern areas, according to *China Daily*.

Desertification means useful land, especially farmland, changes into desert. About 2.6 million square kilometers of China's land is covered with sand. That's about 27% of the country's land. It can also cause sandstorms.

By planting more trees, China cuts its sandstorms by 20%. About 100 square kilometers of land becomes oases(绿洲).

Ian, a British photographer, traveled through northern China last year. He said China changed a lot. And he could see many new oases there.

"It is hard to believe that there used to be desert," he told *Wired* magazine.

(　　)46. What is Ant Forest?

　　A. A big forest.　　B. A group of ants.
　　C. A game.　　D. A match.

(　　)47. What does the underlined word "desertification" in Paragraph 2 mean?

　　A. 赤贫　　B. 暴风雨　　C. 绿化　　D. 荒漠化

(　　)48. Which of the following isn't true?

　　A. There are less oases in China now.
　　B. Land covered with sand cause sandstorms.
　　C. Some of China's land is still covered with sand.
　　D. Chinese have planted lots of trees to stop desertification.

(　　)49. Where does Ian come from?

　　A. America.　　B. Britain.　　C. Australia.　　D. Russia.

(　　)50. What's the best title for the passage?

　　A. How to Play Ant Forest

　　B. How to Stop desertification

　　C. China's Effort to Fight desertification

　　D. A British photographer

C

Fraser Island is in Queensland, Australia, about 200 kilometers north of Brisbane.

It is a very important island because it is completely made of sand, but there is a long beach along the east coast. Planes arrive and leave from here.

The sand makes unusual shapes. There are hills made of sand called sandblows. Nothing grows on them. They move one or two meters a year from the northwest towards the southeast of the island, getting bigger and bigger. At other places on the island, such as Rainbow Gorge, The Cathedral and Red Canyon, the sandy rocks have different colours. Sometimes the rocks are so brown that they turn the sea brown, like coffee.

Surprisingly, the sandy island has a lot of different plants and animals. There are dark forests—eucalyptus woods, beautiful flowers and over a hundred lakes. There are many kinds of birds, like owls and curlews. There are many animals there, too, such as crocodiles, flying foxes and wild dogs called <u>dingoes</u>.

About 50,000 people visit the island every year to see the island's beauty and nature. People enjoy camping and hiking there. Unluckily, the visitors create problems. They damage plants and frighten animals. Their sun cream (防晒霜) makes the water dirty. So it is necessary to manage the visitors. For example, people may not use motor boats or go fishing in the lakes, and they need official papers to drive there.

(　　)51. Fraser Island is a very important island because _____.

　　A. it is made of sand　　　　　　B. it has a long beach

　　C. it is unusual in shape　　　　　D. it has a large airport

(　　)52. Which of the following is True?

　　A. A sandy hill can be formed in a year.

　　B. The sandy hills are red or brown.

　　C. There are lots of people on the sandy hills.

　　D. The sandy hills keep moving.

(　　)53. The underlined word "dingoes" in Paragraph 3 refers to _____.

　　A. crocodiles　　　　　　　　　B. wild dogs

　　C. birds　　　　　　　　　　　　D. flying foxes

(　　)54. From the last paragraph, we can know that _____.

　　A. Fraser Island needs to be protected.

　　B. Fraser Island was serious polluted.

　　C. people will not be allowed to visit Fraser Island.

　　D. plants and animals are in danger on Fraser Island.

(　　)55. The passage is mainly about _____.

　　A. a trip to Fraser Island　　　　B. the life on Fraser Island

　　C. nature on Fraser Island　　　 D. people on Fraser Island

第二节　词义搭配：从(B)栏中选出(A)栏单词的正确解释。(共10分，每小题1分)

(A)	(B)
(　　)56. against	A. become invisible or unnoticeable
(　　)57. battery	B. a glass or plastic vessel for storing liquids
(　　)58. childhood	C. size of the gap between two places
(　　)59. disappear	D. to keep…safe from harm or danger
(　　)60. distance	E. the state of being polluted
(　　)61. drop	F. opposed to, not in favor of
(　　)62. pollution	G. the time of person's life when they are a child
(　　)63. dustbin	H. a sudden sharp decrease in some quantity
(　　)64. bottle	I. a device that produces electricity
(　　)65. protect	J. a bin that holds rubbish until it is collected

第三节　补全对话：根据对话内容，从对话后的选项中选出能填入空白处的最佳选项。(共10分，每小题2分)

A: Good morning, Li Ming! I didn't see you this morning. Where did you go?

B: ___66___

A: What did you do there?

B: ___67___ I was very interested in it.

A: A magazine? ___68___

B: It's about how to protect our environment.

A: ___69___

B: Of course. It tells us to do small things.

A: Yes, that's right. ___70___ Does it mention waste sorting?

B: Yes, it does. Waste sorting is also important. Many things can be recycled and reused.

A: That's really good. Let's start today and do whatever we can to protect our home.

A. What's it about?

B. A small thing can make a big difference in our daily life.

C. I went to the library.

D. I read a magazine there.

E. Does it tell us any good ways?

第三部分　语言技能应用(共分四节，满分 30 分)

第一节　单词拼写：根据下列句子及所给汉语注释，在相应题号后的横线上写出该单词的正确形式。(共 5 分，每小题 1 分)

71. There are 20 votes for him and 5 _____ (反对) him.

72. April is the time to _____ (种植) trees.

73. I have known him from his _____ (童年).

74. Please put the garbage into the _____ (垃圾箱).

75. Don't put plastic dishes in the oven or they will _____ (融化).

第二节　词形变换：用括号内单词的适当形式填空。(共 5 分，每小题 1 分)

76. The passage mainly talks about the _____ (disappear) of polar bears.

77. The number of some wild birds is _____ (drop).

78. I always think about my _____ (child) experiences.

79. We're looking forward to a world of _____ (beautiful) and wonder.

80. Remember it is _____ (recycle) that helps us save the resources.

第三节　改错：从 A、B、C、D 四个画线处找出一处错误的选项，填入括号内，并在横线上写出正确答案。(共 10 分，每小题 2 分)

81. Which picture is showing the harm waste?
　　　　　　　A　　B　　　　C　　　D

82. What can the recycled bottles be make into?
　　　　　　　　A　　　　B　　C　　D

83. There is many air pollution in our city.
　　　A　B　　　C　　　D

84. I use to have a lot of fun in the beautiful environment.
　　A　　　B　　　C　　　D

85. It was in the supermarket where I met my aunt yesterday.
　　A　　　　B　　　　　C　　D

81.(　　)应为_____　82.(　　)应为_____　83.(　　)应为_____

84.(　　)应为_____　85.(　　)应为_____

第四节　书面表达。(共10分)

假如你是李明,你所居住的城市污染很严重,请根据以下要点写一篇短文,说明污染原因,并提出建议,呼吁人们爱护环境、保护家园。

1. 提示词:pollution;worse;cars;rubbish;plant trees;turn off;by bike。

2. 写作要点:(1)污染原因;

　　　　　　(2)环保建议。

3. 注意事项:(1)文中不得出现考生个人的真实信息;

　　　　　　(2)词数:80~100词;

　　　　　　(3)开头已给出,不计入总词数。

How to protect the environment

The environment in my city is becoming worse and worse. ＿＿＿＿＿＿

＿＿＿＿＿＿＿＿＿＿＿＿＿＿＿＿＿＿＿＿＿＿＿＿＿＿＿＿＿＿＿＿＿＿＿＿

＿＿＿＿＿＿＿＿＿＿＿＿＿＿＿＿＿＿＿＿＿＿＿＿＿＿＿＿＿＿＿＿＿＿＿＿

＿＿＿＿＿＿＿＿＿＿＿＿＿＿＿＿＿＿＿＿＿＿＿＿＿＿＿＿＿＿＿＿＿＿＿＿

＿＿＿＿＿＿＿＿＿＿＿＿＿＿＿＿＿＿＿＿＿＿＿＿＿＿＿＿＿＿＿＿＿＿＿＿

＿＿＿＿＿＿＿＿＿＿＿＿＿＿＿＿＿＿＿＿＿＿＿＿＿＿＿＿＿＿＿＿＿＿＿＿

＿＿＿＿＿＿＿＿＿＿＿＿＿＿＿＿＿＿＿＿＿＿＿＿＿＿＿＿＿＿＿＿＿＿＿＿

参考答案

Unit 1　Travel

Warming-up

二、1. 避免　2. comfortable　3. devotion；devote　4. 发现，找到；discovery　5. dynasty
6. marvelous　7. national；nation　8. product；生产　9. 预订；reserve　10. unique
11. 植被　12. experience；experienced

Listening and Speaking

一、1. D　2. C　3. A　4. A　5. D
二、1. A　2. D　3. A　4. B　5. D
三、1. B　2. A　3. C　4. D　5. E

Reading and Writing

一、1. geographer　2. hardships　3. quitting　4. travelling　5. experiences　6. devotion
7. eventually　8. avoided　9. spent　10. died
二、1. A　2. B　3. A　4. D　5. B　6. A　7. A　8. B　9. D　10. C
三、1. B　2. B　3. C　4. C　5. B

Grammar

一、1. A　2. B　3. B　4. C　5. B　6. B　7. D　8. A　9. A　10. A
11. B　12. A　13. B　14. A　15. C　16. A　17. C　18. C　19. B　20. B
21. A　22. B　23. A　24. D　25. C　26. B　27. B　28. A　29. A　30. D
二、1. B 应为 was　2. A 应为 went to　3. A 应为 could　4. B 应为 see　5. A 应为 didn't
6. A 应为 didn't do　7. C 应为 found　8. B 应为 did　9. D 应为 entered
10. C 应为 landed

For Better Performance

一、1. B 2. D 3. B 4. A 5. D

二、1. 各种各样的 2. be famous for 3. give up 4. 值得做 5. 照顾 6. 富于
　　7. 景点 8. pass through 9. set off 10. due to

三、1. geographers 2. gave 3. discovered 4. experienced 5. throughout
　　6. eventually 7. interest 8. excitedly 9. quitting 10. comfortable

四、1. C 应为 finishing 2. D 应为 quitting 3. A 应为 didn't go to 4. B 应为 ask
　　5. D 应为 thousand

单元检测

第一部分　英语知识运用

第一节　1. C 2. C 3. A 4. D 5. B

第二节　6. B 7. B 8. C 9. A 10. D 11. C 12. B 13. A 14. C 15. A
　　　　16. D 17. A 18. C 19. B 20. B 21. D 22. A 23. A 24. D 25. B
　　　　26. D 27. A 28. A 29. D 30. B

第三节　31. A 32. B 33. D 34. C 35. D 36. A 37. D 38. C 39. B 40. A

第二部分　篇章与词汇理解

第一节　41. A 42. A 43. D 44. A 45. C 46. D 47. C 48. A 49. C 50. D
　　　　51. D 52. B 53. B 54. C 55. A

第二节　56. B 57. E 58. F 59. C 60. A 61. G 62. H 63. J 64. I 65. D

第三节　66. C 67. E 68. A 69. D 70. B

第三部分　语言技能应用

第一节　71. devotion 72. unique 73. avoid 74. eventually 75. local

第二节　76. comfortably 77. agencies 78. visiting 79. travelling 80. interested

第三节　81. B 应为 did 82. B 应为 arrived in 83. C 应为 making 84. D 应为 those
　　　　85. B 应为 yourselves

Unit 2　Health and Fitness

Warming-up

二、1. 胃疼 2. 压力下 3. 过敏；反感 4. 喉咙疼 5. 发脾气

6. see a doctor   7. plenty of   8. have a good rest

9. feel tired   10. Ask others for help

Listening and Speaking

一、1. A   2. C   3. D   4. A   5. B

二、1. B   2. A   3. C   4. D   5. E

三、1. E   2. B   3. D   4. C   5. A

Reading and Writing

一、1. active   2. cancer   3. valuable   4. self-respect   5. washing

6. burning   7. development   8. traditional   9. national   10. confident

二、1. A   2. C   3. B   4. D   5. C   6. C   7. D   8. C   9. A   10. B

三、1. C   2. D   3. A   4. B   5. D

Grammar

一、1. C   2. D   3. B   4. B   5. C   6. B   7. D   8. A   9. C   10. C

11. B   12. C   13. D   14. C   15. A   16. C   17. A   18. A   19. A   20. A

21. C   22. C   23. D   24. B   25. C   26. B   27. A   28. D   29. C   30. A

二、1. B 应为 are   2. A 应为 is   3. C 应为 on   4. C 应为 have   5. B 应为 steal

6. D 应为 to be done   7. B 应为 have ignored   8. A 应为 will get

9. C 应为 harm   10. A 应为 learning

For Better Performance

一、1. A   2. C   3. C   4. A   5. B

二、1. 公共运输   2. 作为……结果   3. 帮某人一个忙   4. 洗衣机

5. 走来走去   6. burn off   7. lose one's temper

8. what's more   9. suffer from   10. recover from

三、1. appointment   2. traditional   3. communication   4. truth   5. development

6. valuable   7. physical   8. activities   9. experienced   10. healthy

四、1. A 应为 much   2. C 应为 eating   3. C 应为 living   4. C 应为 feels

5. C 应为 to finish

英语2同步练习(基础模块)

单元检测

第一部分　英语知识运用

第一节　1. A　2. C　3. C　4. A　5. B

第二节　6. A　7. C　8. C　9. B　10. A　11. A　12. B　13. B　14. B　15. C
　　　　16. A　17. C　18. A　19. B　20. B　21. D　22. A　23. B　24. B　25. A
　　　　26. B　27. C　28. B　29. A　30. D

第三节　31. C　32. A　33. A　34. B　35. C　36. D　37. D　38. A　39. C　40. B

第二部分　篇章与词汇理解

第一节　41. C　42. B　43. C　44. D　45. A　46. D　47. B　48. A　49. D　50. C
　　　　51. B　52. D　53. D　54. A　55. C

第二节　56. D　57. B　58. I　59. A　60. G　61. F　62. E　63. J　64. C　65. H

第三节　66. C　67. D　68. B　69. E　70. A

第三部分　语言技能应用

第一节　71. pressure　72. effort　73. temper　74. depression　75. technician

第二节　76. development　77. traditional　78. activities　79. physical　80. appointment

第三节　81. C 应为 have　82. C 应为 none　83. B 应为 is　84. B 应为 it
　　　　85. C 应为 should be

Unit 3　Internship

Warming-up

二、1. 三方协议　2. agreement; agree　3. 实地考察　4. 培训;教员;实习生
　　5. 实习计划　6. 实习档案　7. preschool teacher　8. auto mechanic
　　9. waiter/waitress　10. kindergarten

Listening and Speaking

一、1. B　2. A　3. C　4. A　5. D

二、1. B　2. C　3. E　4. A　5. D

三、1. C　2. A　3. D　4. E　5. B

Reading and Writing

一、1. majors　2. succeed　3. dreaming　4. Challenges　5. qualified

— 4 —

6. disagree　7. expectation　8. education　9. founded　10. providing

二、1. B　2. A　3. C　4. A　5. C　6. A　7. B　8. A　9. C　10. B

三、1. B　2. C　3. D　4. B　5. C

Grammar

一、1. A　2. D　3. A　4. B　5. D　6. C　7. D　8. D　9. A　10. D
11. B　12. A　13. A　14. B　15. A　16. D　17. C　18. B　19. A　20. C
21. B　22. C　23. D　24. C　25. C　26. C　27. D　28. A　29. B　30. B

二、1. B 应为 was　2. B 应为 was watching　3. B 应为 before long
4. C 应为 are watching　5. C 应为 moves　6. A 应为 are living　7. B 应为 was
8. D 应为 rains　9. B 应为 plays　10. B 应为 was doing

For Better Performance

一、1. A　2. B　3. D　4. B　5. D

二、1. 合格的　2. 步骤　3. 签署　4. 奖学金　5. 接到；收到　6. challenge
7. assistant　8. express　9. intern　10. description

三、1. expressions　2. description　3. challenging　4. decision　5. excellent
6. instruction　7. organization　8. agreement　9. Knowledge　10. service

四、1. C 应为 taken　2. C 应为 with　3. C 应为 showing
4. B 应为 is　5. D 应为 brother's

单元检测

第一部分　英语知识运用

第一节　1. A　2. D　3. B　4. C　5. A

第二节　6. B　7. C　8. A　9. C　10. A　11. C　12. C　13. A　14. B　15. B
16. D　17. B　18. A　19. B　20. C　21. A　22. C　23. A　24. A　25. C
26. C　27. C　28. B　29. A　30. A

第三节　31. B　32. A　33. C　34. A　35. B　36. C　37. D　38. A　39. A　40. C

第二部分　篇章与词汇理解

第一节　41. C　42. D　43. C　44. B　45. D
46. D　47. A　48. B　49. C　50. C
51. B　52. D　53. A　54. C　55. C

第二节　56. C　57. D　58. B　59. E　60. I　61. H　62. A　63. F　64. G　65. J

第三节　66. E　67. A　68. D　69. B　70. C

第三部分　语言技能运用

第一节　71. colleagues　72. description　73. pre-service　74. progress　75. solving

第二节　76. preparation　77. beginning　78. waiting　79. amazed　80. valuable

第三节　81. C 应为 high　82. C 应为 go　83. D 应为 to　84. C 应为 showing

85. C 应为 was founded

Unit 4　Volunteer Work

Warming-up

二、1. ferry　2. 轻轨　3. 海滩　4. contribute　5. architecture
6. 电子　7. exhibit　8. 知识　9. 位置　10. 公共

Listening and Speaking

一、1. B　2. A　3. A　4. D　5. C

二、1. A　2. B　3. C　4. D　5. E

三、1. D　2. C　3. A　4. B　5. E

Reading and Writing

一、1. home and abroad　2. look forward to　3. major in　4. act as　5. be skilled in
6. apply　7. responsible　8. organization　9. history　10. contribute

二、1. D　2. A　3. B　4. C　5. B　6. D　7. A　8. C　9. A　10. C

三、1. A　2. B　3. C　4. D　5. A

Grammar

一、1. A　2. B　3. B　4. A　5. A　6. D　7. B　8. A　9. D　10. C
11. C　12. C　13. A　14. A　15. C　16. C　17. C　18. A　19. C　20. D
21. D　22. D　23. B　24. D　25. D　26. B　27. B　28. C　29. A　30. B

二、1. B 应为 home　2. A 应为 wasn't　3. D 应为 safety　4. C 应为 get / have / receive
5. B 应为 to do　6. on 应为 in　7. B 应为 is　8. B 应为 were watching
9. A 应为 so　10. A 应为 be

For Better Performance

一、1. B　2. B　3. A　4. D　5. C

二、1. 平民的 2. knowledge 3. activity 4. 后果 5. 专业
　　6. 王宫 7. 熟练掌握 8. act as 9. organization 10. basic education

三、1. elementary 2. helpful 3. participation 4. written 5. International
　　6. useful 7. cultural 8. volunteers 9. themselves 10. knees

四、1. C 应为 that/which 或去掉 where 2. B 应为放在 looking 后面 3. B 应为 whom
　　4. B 应为 which 5. C 应为 which

单元检测

第一部分　英语知识运用

第一节　1. A 2. D 3. C 4. A 5. B
第二节　6. B 7. C 8. C 9. B 10. A 11. A 12. B 13. A 14. D 15. B
　　　　16. B 17. B 18. A 19. B 20. B 21. C 22. C 23. C 24. A 25. B
　　　　26. D 27. D 28. B 29. A 30. B
第三节　31. A 32. C 33. D 34. C 35. C 36. B 37. A 38. D 39. A 40. B

第二部分　篇章与词汇理解

第一节　41. C 42. A 43. B 44. D 45. C 46. B 47. C 48. C 49. C 50. D
　　　　51. C 52. A 53. C 54. D 55. D
第二节　56. C 57. I 58. H 59. E 60. A 61. J 62. D 63. F 64. G 65. B
第三节　66. C 67. E 68. D 69. A 70. B

第三部分　语言技能应用

第一节　71. purpose 72. injured 73. active 74. native 75. forecast
第二节　76. thanked 77. hitting 78. ridden 79. cut 80. shown
第三节　81. A 应为 herself 82. D 应为 ninth 83. B 应为 to work 84. C 应为 lets
　　　　85. C 应为去掉 so

Unit 5　Ancient Civilization

Warming-up

二、1. 真实的；actually 2. 艺术家 3. attract；attractive 4. 文字
　　5. civilization 6. 好奇的；curiosity 7. exchange
　　8. 展览 9. impress；impression 10. 财宝

— 7 —

Listening and Speaking

一、1. A   2. D   3. C   4. D   5. B

二、1. C   2. D   3. A   4. E   5. B

三、1. C   2. E   3. B   4. D   5. A

Reading and Writing

一、1. exhibition   2. actual   3. western   4. maritime   5. emissary
　　6. paintings   7. memory   8. lively   9. attractive   10. civilization

二、1. C   2. B   3. D   4. A   5. B   6. B   7. C   8. A   9. D   10. C

三、1. D   2. C   3. B   4. B   5. A

Grammar

一、1. B   2. D   3. D   4. A   5. D   6. C   7. C   8. C   9. A   10. D
　　11. A   12. A   13. B   14. D   15. B   16. A   17. A   18. B   19. C   20. D
　　21. D   22. B   23. C   24. C   25. B   26. A   27. C   28. B   29. D   30. B

二、1. C 应为 he can   2. C 应为 what   3. C 应为 was   4. C 应为 John asked
　　5. C 应为 whether   6. D 应为 I put   7. B 应为 travels   8. D 应为 would
　　9. C 应为 goes   10. C 应为 how

For Better Performance

一、1. C   2. C   3. D   4. A   5. B

二、1. 早在……的时候   2. attract to   3. China fever   4. 追溯到   5. 寻找
　　6. 奥林匹克运动会   7. 丝绸之路   8. neither…nor…   9. what's more
　　10. at that time

三、1. Spanish   2. actually   3. exchanges   4. peak   5. artist
　　6. curious   7. century   8. treasure   9. boost   10. route

四、1. D 应为 as early as   2. D 应为 is   3. B 应为 was
　　4. D 应为 you were waiting for   5. C 应为 are

单元检测

第一部分　英语知识运用

第一节   1. C   2. A   3. B   4. D   5. B

第二节   6. A   7. C   8. A   9. C   10. D   11. A   12. B   13. C   14. D   15. B

|第三节| 16. C 17. C 18. C 19. C 20. A 21. A 22. B 23. C 24. B 25. D
26. A 27. B 28. C 29. A 30. C

第三节 31. B 32. D 33. B 34. A 35. C 36. B 37. C 38. D 39. D 40. D

第二部分　篇章与词汇理解

第一节 41. D 42. B 43. A 44. C 45. D 46. C 47. D 48. A 49. C 50. B
51. B 52. D 53. D 54. C 55. A

第二节 56. G 57. I 58. F 59. A 60. J 61. H 62. E 63. B 64. D 65. C

第三节 66. B 67. E 68. C 69. A 70. D

第三部分　语言技能应用

第一节 71. technology 72. vitality 73. portrait 74. enlighten 75. characters

第二节 76. reporters 77. explorer 78. exhibition 79. sculptor 80. Cultural

第三节 81. D 应为 for   82. D 应为 wonders   83. B 应为 impress   84. D 应为 is
85. C 应为 sent

Unit 6　Craftsmanship

Warming-up

二、1. 雕木　2. 品质　3. 焊接钢　4. 设计　5. 钟表匠　6. creative
7. persistent　8. craftsmanship　9. warm-hearted　10. hard-working

Listening and Speaking

一、1. D 2. A 3. B 4. C 5. A

二、1. D 2. A 3. B 4. B 5. A

三、1. B 2. C 3. A 4. E 5. D

Reading and Writing

一、1. craftsmanship　2. butcher　3. equipment　4. preparing　5. standard
6. creative　7. fashionable　8. patience　9. achievement　10. perfection

二、1. C 2. B 3. A 4. D 5. D 6. B 7. C 8. A 9. B 10. C

三、1. D 2. D 3. C 4. C 5. B

Grammar

一、1. D 2. B 3. B 4. C 5. D 6. C 7. B 8. A 9. B 10. C

英语2 同步练习(基础模块)

11. B   12. B   13. A   14. B   15. C   16. A   17. B   18. D   19. B   20. A
21. C   22. C   23. B   24. C   25. C   26. A   27. C   28. B   29. C   30. D

二、1. A 应为 was told   2. B 应为 look   3. C 应为 take   4. B 应为 will be built
5. D 应为 watering   6. C 应为 were   7. B 应为 not   8. A 应为 amazed
9. B 应为 to play   10. B 应为 feels

For Better Performance

一、1. A   2. C   3. A   4. D   5. C

二、1. 从前   2. 既不……也不……   3. 最后   4. 被认为   5. 关心   6. be connected to
7. focus on   8. take up   9. strive for   10. from generation to generation

三、1. achievement   2. friendly   3. disappointed   4. creative   5. designer
6. importance   7. production   8. fashionable   9. patience   10. excellence

四、1. D 应为 swimming   2. C 应为 continued   3. C 应为 are believed
4. A 应为 a funny   5. D 应为 importance

单元检测

第一部分　英语知识运用

第一节   1. B   2. A   3. D   4. B   5. B

第二节   6. C   7. D   8. A   9. D   10. A   11. B   12. C   13. C   14. C   15. A
16. B   17. A   18. A   19. B   20. A   21. A   22. B   23. A   24. C   25. B
26. C   27. B   28. B   29. B   30. A

第三节   31. B   32. D   33. A   34. A   35. C   36. C   37. A   38. B   39. A   40. D

第二部分　篇章与词汇理解

第一节   41. D   42. B   43. A   44. C   45. C   46. B   47. D   48. C   49. A   50. C
51. A   52. C   53. C   54. C   55. D

第二节   56. F   57. G   58. A   59. J   60. C   61. D   62. H   63. I   64. E   65. B

第三节   66. C   67. B   68. E   69. A   70. D

第三部分　语言技能应用

第一节   71. amazing   72. graceful   73. quality   74. impressive   75. persistent
第二节   76. preparation   77. achievement   78. movement   79. difference
80. importance
第三节   81. B 应为 such   82. A 应为 Who   83. C 应为 not to
84. C 应为 is being planned   85. A 应为 what

Unit 7　Invention and Innovation

Warming-up

二、1. 蓝牙　2. drone　3. 无线网　4. smart watch　5. 3D 打印机
　　6. virtual reality（VR）　7. 网络　8. computer　9. 发明　10. innovation

Listening and Speaking

一、1. C　2. D　3. A　4. B　5. A

二、1. D　2. E　3. B　4. A　5. C

三、1. A　2. C　3. E　4. D　5. B

Reading and Writing

一、1. Technology　2. doubtful　3. surrounded　4. allows　5. secure
　　6. benefiting　7. self-driving　8. Online　9. Internet　10. Smart

二、1. D　2. C　3. A　4. B　5. A　6. D　7. B　8. A　9. C　10. C

三、1. C　2. A　3. C　4. B　5. D

Grammar

一、1. D　2. A　3. D　4. C　5. B　6. C　7. A　8. D　9. B　10. C
　　11. A　12. B　13. D　14. A　15. C　16. C　17. B　18. A　19. C　20. A
　　21. D　22. C　23. B　24. A　25. C　26. A　27. B　28. C　29. A　30. D

二、1. C 应为 so　2. B 应为 and　3. A 应为/　4. C 应为 or　5. B 应为 so
　　6. C 应为 have to　7. B 应为 but　8. B 应为 but　9. D 应为 it　10. D 应为 joined

For Better Performance

一、1. D　2. C　3. A　4. B　5. C

二、1. 发明　2. economy　3. 距离　4. politics　5. 发展
　　6. culture　7. 在 21 世纪早期　8. dream of　9. 在那时候　10. allow sb.to do sth

三、1. inventions　2. robot　3. operate　4. guaranteed　5. Internet

6. connected   7. dreamed   8. distances   9. bulb   10. space

四、1. B 应为 have been   2. D 应为 heavy   3. C 应为 greatly   4. C 应为 but
　　5. A 应为 including

单元检测

第一部分　英语知识运用

第一节　1. A   2. B   3. D   4. C   5. B

第二节　6. B   7. A   8. C   9. D   10. A   11. C   12. B   13. A   14. C   15. A
　　　　16. C   17. A   18. D   19. B   20. D   21. A   22. A   23. D   24. C   25. A
　　　　26. D   27. B   28. B   29. C   30. A

第三节　31. A   32. B   3. D   34. B   35. A   36. C   37. A   38. C   39. D   40. B

第二部分　篇章与词汇理解

第一节　41. A   42. C   43. B   44. D   45. B   46. A   47. C   48. D   49. C   50. B
　　　　51. B   52. B   53. C   54. D   55. D

第二节　56. C   57. G   58. F   59. A   60. H   61. B   62. I   63. D   64. J   65. E

第三节　66. D   67. A   68. C   69. E   70. B

第三部分　语言技能应用

第一节　71. benefit   72. customer   73. delivery   74. feature   75. function

第二节　76. guarantee   77. introduce   78. operate   79. pests   80. prefer

第三节　81. B 应为 managed   82. B 应为 easy   83. C 应为 interested
　　　　84. C 应为 that/which   85. C 应为 high

Unit 8　Green Earth

Warming-up

二、1. 融化   2. plastic   3. 污染   4. smog   5. 北极   6. polar bear
　　7. 冰   8. destroy   9. 布袋子   10. global warming   11. 垃圾分类   12. take place

Listening and Speaking

一、1. D   2. A   3. B   4. D   5. C

二、1. C　2. E　3. D　4. A　5. B

三、1. D　2. C　3. E　4. B　5. A

Reading and Writing

一、1. dustbins　2. bottles　3. dropping　4. bears　5. handbook
　　6. recycled　7. global　8. protect　9. garbage　10. generate

二、1. A　2. D　3. B　4. C　5. B　6. A　7. C　8. B　9. A　10. D

三、1. C　2. D　3. A　4. B　5. D

Grammar

一、1. A　2. C　3. B　4. D　5. C　6. A　7. D　8. B　9. B　10. A
　　11. C　12. D　13. A　14. B　15. D　16. A　17. B　18. D　19. C　20. B
　　21. A　22. C　23. D　24. A　25. D　26. C　27. B　28. D　29. B　30. A

二、1. D 应为 is　2. C 应为 that　3. A 应为 It　4. B 应为 him　5. C 应为 that
　　6. C 应为 helps　7. B 应为 on October 1st　8. B 应为 with　9. D 应为 met
　　10. C 应为 saw

For Better Performance

一、1. C　2. B　3. C　4. D　5. A

二、1. 意识到　2. protect　3. 号召　4. turn off　5. 以这种方式
　　6. pay attention to　7. 全世界　8. up to　9. 例如　10. take part in

三、1. realize　2. turn　3. attention　4. part　5. special
　　6. survey　7. discuss　8. changing　9. global　10. importance

四、1. B 应为 taking　2. C 应为 that　3. B 应为 four-step　4. A 应为 It　5. C 应为 reduce

单元检测

第一部分　英语知识运用

第一节　1. D　2. C　3. B　4. A　5. C

第二节　6. B　7. D　8. B　9. A　10. B　11. C　12. D　13. B　14. C　15. B
　　　　16. C　17. A　18. D　19. B　20. D　21. A　22. B　23. D　24. C　25. A
　　　　26. D　27. B　28. D　29. B　30. A

第三节　31. B　32. C　3. A　34. C　35. D　36. A　37. B　38. C　39. D　40. A

— 13 —

第二部分　篇章与词汇理解

第一节　41. C　42. A　43. B　44. B　45. D　46. C　47. D　48. A　49. B　50. C
　　　　51. A　52. D　53. B　54. A　55. C

第二节　56. F　57. I　58. G　59. A　60. C　61. H　62. E　63. J　64. B　65. D

第三节　66. C　67. D　68. A　69. E　70. B

第三部分　语言技能应用

第一节　71. against　72. plant　73. childhood　74. dustbin　75. melt

第二节　76. disappearance　77. dropping　78. childhood　79. beauty　80. recycling

第三节　81. C 应为 harmful　82. C 应为 made　83. B 应为 much　84. A 应为 used to
　　　　85. C 应为 that